Adele Marion Fielde

Pagoda Shadows

Studies from Life in China

Adele Marion Fielde

Pagoda Shadows
Studies from Life in China

ISBN/EAN: 9783337166830

Printed in Europe, USA, Canada, Australia, Japan

Cover: Foto ©Andreas Hilbeck / pixelio.de

More available books at **www.hansebooks.com**

PAGODA SHADOWS:

Studies from Life in China.

BY
ADELE M. FIELDE.

*WITH AN INTRODUCTION BY
J. OSWALD DYKES, D.D.*

T. OGILVIE SMITH,
14, PATERNOSTER SQUARE, LONDON.
1887.

Butler & Tanner,
The Selwood Printing Works,
Frome, and London.

PREFACE.

THESE studies have been made during a residence of ten years in China, with a knowledge of the language of the people, and an opportunity for close observation of their social customs. The autobiographies and the stories are exact translations of verbal narrations given to the author in the Swatow dialect.

A. M. F.

SWATOW, CHINA, 1887.

INTRODUCTION.

THE conversion of China is the heaviest piece of work now left for the Church of Christ to do. Nowhere else on the globe does there exist a compact or homogeneous population of anything like the same extent. The future Church of China will be in mere bulk the greatest branch ever known of the Church universal. But its importance will not be measured by its bulk alone. The Chinese are pretty sure to have a main part to play in the future of Asia. Those who possess the best acquaintance with the farther East, or are best able to forecast its probable development, are of opinion that this swarming Chinese stock, patient, industrious, frugal, ready to migrate, and able to thrive where others starve, is destined to be (next, perhaps, to the Anglo-American) a predominant element in the lands that are washed by the Pacific Ocean.

It used to be said that China contained one-third of the human family. Since interior Africa has been found to be populous, our conceptions of the human family have become enlarged. It is also to be recollected that the best estimate we can form of the population of China itself can be only an approximate one. We lack the materials, therefore, for such a comparison. But, be its proportion to the earth's total population what it may, it is certain that China counts its people by hundreds of millions. The difficulty of reaching such a vast population so as to change its immemorial beliefs would be prodigious, even were it less stationary or inflexible than it has hitherto shown itself. Fortunately there are certain favouring circumstances which serve to lighten the task. The whole country is most densely occupied. Men stand closely grouped, so that each convert gained touches and affects a crowd of neighbours. Though people do not move far from home, yet a network of land and water highways offers ready, if leisurely, means of communication. In this way its provinces can be traversed from end to end. Society coheres tightly together, social bonds being singularly strong. Hence custom and public opinion are nearly omnipotent. So long as these remain anti-Christian, no doubt they constitute a formidable barrier to change. But for the same reason, once custom and opinion begin to turn, the change will be rapid; for an organized community ruled by usage, when it moves at all, moves in a body. In a similar way, the dominant influence of the great official or literary order, which is the chief bulwark of heathenism and is likely to be so for some time, will operate as decisively in favour of a new creed so soon as the *literati* themselves become open to Western thought. That this must come no one doubts. That it may come sooner than used to be supposed is even growing probable. Indications thicken that the old blind antagonism to foreign ways begins to yield. The instance of the Marquis Tseng shows how open to European ideas are some at least of the highest minds in the Empire. Two twin forces, commerce and diplomatic intercourse, are surely

Introduction. ix

breaking up the iron-bound conservatism of ancient China. For it, too, a new world begins. And this means the breaking up of a path for the kingdom of God.

More than by any other single circumstance, our task will be lightened by the fact that half the men of China are able to read, and that from one end of it to another educated men understand the same printed page. There is here an engine of enormous force ready to our hand. It is as if, at the Reformation, Latin had been familiar, not only to a few scholars in each European nation, but to half the male population of Europe. There is absolutely no obstacle to the flooding of China with Christian teaching through the press, save the absence of any Christian literature to circulate, or the indisposition of the learned to peruse it. The creation of a Christian literature in Chinese is an urgent work calling for a host of scholarly labourers. For it is quite on the cards that educated China may become willing to read our books before we have the books to give them. Already this vast reading public is learning to value those handbooks in European science which are accessible. Within a few years more it will probably welcome, or at least tolerate, the direct teaching of our faith by works avowedly Christian.

In spite of advantages such as these, which afford us a reasonable prospect of ultimate success, the conversion of China remains a herculean labour. For generations to come it is likely to task the strength of Churches both in Europe and America—indeed, both of Papal and Protestant Christendom. As yet we have scarce brushed the fringe of the gigantic Empire. A territory so wide will have to be pierced and traversed along a hundred routes. Before its thickset villages and myriad-peopled cities can be overtaken, every description of agency will need to be put in operation. Especially must a native agency be called into existence far more numerous than the foreign missionaries, and far less costly. The women, too, can only be reached in detail and by women, which means a whole army of humble Bible-women scattered over the face of the country. In short, the leavening work must needs be gradual, slow even, done by such persistent plodding as recalls the best qualities of John Chinaman himself. It is sure to be best done by natives. Of the material available for work of this patient sort, at least among female converts, and of the use to be made of it, a good deal will be found in this little work that is most instructive. How long the process of sapping and mining must go on before anything like a religious revolution occurs in China, no one at present seems able to form a guess. Probably for a great while to come. But that a crisis is sure to follow may be safely predicted. We dare not count on any easy victory. It is not in the least likely that ancestral superstitions which hold so ancient and firm a seat, which are moreover tight locked in with a vast system of bureaucratic government, will yield without a struggle. The struggle may not improbably convulse Chinese society one day; it may even drench its soil with blood.

It is in no holiday spirit that the Christian Church ought to address itself to an enterprise like this. Rather should it be faced with set teeth and a tightened girdle. Far greater sacrifices will have to be made for it than we are yet dreaming of. The needs of China will have to sit heavier on the consciences of our children than they do on our own. Meantime, everything should be welcomed which helps to bring that far-off land nearer to

Introduction. xi

our hearts, which assists us to understand it better, or quickens our sympathy with the life of its people. For men's interest is to be reached through their imaginations. What we realize dimly moves us but a little. To beget and to sustain a deeper concern for missionary work in China, it is indispensable that the average Christian at home should be enabled to transport himself in fancy to the rice-field or the tea-farm which the peasants till, to canals bright with colour and busy with traffic-boats, to the narrow city street, where, in squalid homes, men and women in cotton frocks crowd and toil in endless masses, where they live and die. We want not so much statistics as details of every-day life. It is well that the number of baptisms should figure in an annual report, or the growth of each new "station" be narrated in the monthly letter home; but such information needs to be supplemented. We want to know just how these same heathen exist. We long for scenes of home-life; for tales that will set the people before us in their habit as they move; for some one to reproduce for us the private experience of human beings whose joys and sorrows after all are like our own, in spite of their slit eyes and pigtail behind. It is true they are a queer folk, with an odd, far-away look about them, which rather repels than invites English sympathy. Even these quaint traits, however, may be made to seize the more upon one's imagination, if only they get to be associated with a veritable human soul, like one's own in its tragedies and comedies. Only it must be by ones and twos we get to know them. There are so many of them, that in the mass they rather oppress one. They look, too, from our remote point of vision, wonderfully alike; and the imagination gets lost in a wearisome crowd, all of the same pattern, blue-frocked and pigtailed. Hence one longs to get close alongside the Chinaman, as "a man and a brother," feeling through the blue blouse the beating of the same unchanging human heart.

It is in this way that Miss Fielde's unpretending little book appears to me likely to do real service here in England, as already it has done in America. Just because it is unpretending, and homely, and natural; because there is nothing at all sensational about it, nor any effort at fine writing; because it is neither a mission report, nor a book of travels, nor a treatise with the least pretension to completeness, but simply a handful of very short sketches, quite miscellaneous and easily read, full of details of real life and simple stories about real people:—therefore it may help to win some readers to a kinder and more human interest in the Chinese people. "I hope," said Joseph Cook, when he first introduced the little book to the American public—"I hope that a near view of China, such as she gives, may affect others as it did me." Yes; it is the "near view" we want to get. Of such books we can hardly have too many, and we have very few. One sometimes wishes that missionaries (along with other and higher qualities) carried more observant eyes, or wielded a more graphic pen. When foreign sights and sounds have grown so familiar to them as to awaken no fresh interest in their own minds, they forget how unfamiliar these things remain for us. It is a happy faculty which, after years of residence among a people, is still quick to note and skilful to record whatever their life contains of the genuine picturesque—still more, whatever it offers that can stir in far-off readers under other skies the pulses of a genuine human sympathy. This Miss Fielde has been able to do for her

Introduction. xiii

Christian sisters whom she has been training to work for Christ among their countrywomen. Nothing more true to native experience in humble villages can well be imagined than their narratives as she has set them down for us. Her volume makes thus a real addition to our China Mission literature and to our practical acquaintance with that mighty people, whom we Westerns mean to convert to the Gospel of our Lord and Saviour. In Jesus are Chinese and English hands already locked together, and in Jesus shall East and West grow ever more and more into One Body.

CONTENTS.

CHAPTER		PAGE
I.	THE STATUS OF WOMAN	1
II.	CHILD-LIFE IN CATHAY: THE STORY OF NUMBER FOUR	9
III.	THE EXTENT OF A GREAT CRIME	19
IV.	FOOT-BINDING	27
V.	AN ESPOUSAL	33
VI.	THE INVISIBLE BRIDEGROOM	40
VII.	HABITATIONS	43
VIII.	THE INCONVENIENCE OF HEATHENISM	47
IX.	SPIRITUALISM	57
X.	THE KITCHEN-GOD	61
XI.	THE INFLUENCE OF THE IDOLS	64
XII.	THE STONE PRINCESS AND HER TRAIN	68
XIII.	BUDDHIST NUNS	72
XIV.	LOAN ASSOCIATIONS	75
XV.	OUR APOTHECARY	77
XVI.	RAMBLINGS	80
XVII.	NATIVE FEMALE EVANGELISTS	91
XVIII.	BIOGRAPHY OF LITTLE GALE	100
XIX.	THE AUTOBIOGRAPHY OF AUNT LUCK	104

CHAPTER		PAGE
XX.	The Story of Speed and the Bamboo Dragon	108
XXI.	Gold Getter	113
XXII.	Keepsake	117
XXIII.	Orchid Loses seven-tenths of her Sorrow	124
XXIV.	Love's Purposes	128
XXV.	One Night's Work	132
XXVI.	The Herb that Grew on a Pirate Island	135
XXVII.	Tapestry	138
XXVIII.	Out of the Depths	143
XXIX.	The Mists of Morning	149
XXX.	Light at Eventide	154
XXXI.	How a Familiar Spirit was Ejected from a Household. — The Story Told by Tolerance	160
XXXII.	The Pillars of the Church at South Spur	167
XXXIII.	Silver Flower's Account of Herself	179
XXXIV.	Language, Literature, and Folk-lore	191
XXXV.	The Sphere of Women's Work in China	203

PAGODA SHADOWS.

CHAPTER I.

THE STATUS OF WOMAN.

LIFE, in China, is a stern thing for both men and women; but, as in all places where Christ is not, the heaviest burdens are put upon the weakest. The Chinese woman does not walk in the street with her husband; she does not eat with him, but takes what is left after the men of the family have finished their meal; she has no legal right to anything whatever, apart from her male relatives. Yet her condition is, in some respects, better than that of her sisters in neighbouring countries. She is not a sufferer through any system of caste, as in India; she is not shut up in a harem, as in Turkey; she is not denied the possession of a soul and the religious privileges of men, as in Burma; she is not degraded by polyandry, as in Thibet; she is not in a climate which keeps her bare and lazy, like the women of Siam. Her virtue is as carefully guarded and as highly esteemed as in any country in the world. Female children and elderly women associate with persons of the same age and of the other sex, on terms of apparent equality. Girls, though not kept in such seclusion as in India, do not go out alone, nor appear before male visitors. The Chinese give woman all the social freedom that is discreet for her in a land where the cleansing and controlling power of Christian principle is unknown.

In a country where extortion is the chief use of office, and fear of it the main spur to obedience, neither women nor men claim political rights. But there is no law preventing women from following any occupation in which they may be skilled.

The attainments of women in literature are much lauded and respected. Practically, such attainments are uncommon; but historians refer with pride to the scholarship of a few, and novelists are fond of representing their heroines as skilled in writing both poetry and prose. Knowing writers about China tell us eloquently and truly of its system for the examination and promotion of scholars, and lead one to infer that education is nearly universal. In almost every village there is a private school in which a few boys are taught to read; but the proportion of those taught is very small, and native girls' schools are almost unknown. Of the men, not more than one in a hundred can read; and of women, I have seen few outside the Christian mission-schools who could read, except those despised little girls who act in theatres. In the whole empire, probably not more than one woman in a thousand knows how to read.

For acts of heroism or for exalted virtue a woman may, like men, have an honorary portal erected for her with the emperor's sanction. She may even aspire to deification, since many of the richest and most popular temples are those of the Queen of Heaven, the Protector of Sailors, and of other goddesses who were once earthly women.

In one thing the Chinese woman is exceptionally

blessed. She has inherited from former generations a style of dress at once modest, economical, healthful, and becoming. It covers the whole person, and unlike many Western costumes, which make more noticeable what they profess to conceal, it shields the contour of the body from observation. It takes but eight yards of yard-wide cloth for a complete suit of winter garments; and there is no waste in cutting nor in unnecessary appendages. Its truest economy, however, is in that saving of mental worry which comes from always cutting by the same pattern, and in obviating all need of fitting. It allows unrestricted play to every muscle, is of the same thickness over the whole body, is not in the way when at work, and it has little weight while it has all needful warmth.

Children are sometimes betrothed in infancy, but as betrothal is as binding as marriage, the Chinese have learned wisdom, and usually defer it until a year or two before the marriage, which takes place when the girl is about fifteen.

The proposals of betrothal are made by the parents of the young man, through a matrimonial agent or go-between, whose business it is to know the history and expectations of the marriageable people of the neighbourhood. Sometimes the selection of the bride is left wholly to the go-between, and sometimes she simply carries messages between the parents who have formed their plans previously. The betrothal is often made without either of the persons concerned being aware of what is being done on their behalf, and the bride is brought to her husband's home without ever having seen him or any member of his family. Having arrived there, she is at once incorporated in her father-in-law's household, and thenceforth has little association with her own kin. Her happiness depends more on the character of her mother-in-law than on that of her husband, for by her husband's mother and grandmother she is wholly ruled. She is domestic servant for the whole household, and especial waiting-maid to her mother-in-law. Sometimes very strong attachments are formed between these women. I have seen a woman weep at being separated for a time from her mother-in-law, and express no pleasure when told that her husband was coming to see her. On the other hand, there is often tyranny on the part of the elder woman, and dislike on that of the younger one.

The wife may be divorced for scolding, barrenness, lasciviousness, leprosy, disobedience to her husband's parents, and thieving; but all these causes are null when her parents are not alive to receive her back again. A man cannot have more than one wife, but he may take concubines, whose children are legally subject to the authority of the wife, as Bilhah's were to Rachel. Public opinion does not, however, justify the taking of a concubine except when the wife has borne no sons. In regions where the people are very poor, it is uncommon for a man to have more than one wife.

A husband may beat his wife to death, and go unpunished; but a wife who strikes her husband a single blow may be divorced, and beaten a hundred blows with the heavy bamboo.

As long as a woman is childless, she serves; as soon as she becomes a mother, she begins to rule, and her dominion increases perpetually with the number of her descendants and the diminution of her elders. Married at fifteen, she is often a great-grandmother at sixty, and the head of a household of some dozens of persons.

The Status of Woman. 5

So greatly does the welfare of the wife depend on her having sons, that it is not strange that they are her greatest desire, and her chief pride. For them she will sacrifice all else. Her daughters leave her and become legally and truly an integral part of another family for ever. For domestic service, care in sickness, help in old age, and offerings for the sustenance of her spirit after death, she must rely on her son's wife, while her own daughter performs these services for someone else. The prosperity of a Chinese household is in proportion to the number of its sons.

A widow usually remains in her father-in-law's house, sharing the food and labour of the family, being as much a part of the household as before her husband's death. Though ever so young, a second marriage would bring reproach and disgrace. Unlike an Israelite, she cannot legally marry one of her husband's brothers, nor any person of the same surname. If childless, she may adopt sons, who may inherit her husband's property as surely as would his own offspring; but should she marry afterward, the estate reverts to her husband's brothers.

She is apt to remain in widowhood if there be rice-fields affording her a living, unless she be driven to marry by the persecutions of her brothers-in-law. A sad case occurred in 1875 in Kit-ie. The widow was twenty-seven years old, and had a son aged ten. Her husband had been dead six years. His parents had both died before him, and their property had been divided lawfully and equally among their five sons, so that each owned a bit of land and a room in the ancestral home. This widow continued to live in her husband's house, supporting herself and her child by the cultivation of the land, taking care of the household gear, and looking forward to her son's manhood. But her husband's brothers wanted the property and the boy, and tried to persuade her to enter a Buddhist nunnery. She refused, and was continually persecuted. There is no law for Chinese women so plain as the law that they shall obey their elders; and, wearied out by her troubles, she at last visited some Buddhist retreats with a view to becoming a recluse; but she was so disgusted by what she saw, that she resolved more firmly than ever not to leave her home. Just then she heard that in a neighbouring village, a new and good doctrine was taught, and the next Sunday she went some miles to hear a Christian sermon. On her return her brothers-in-law reviled her, saying that she had been away seeking a husband. The next day they sold her for a sum amounting to nearly twenty pounds, to an old man in another village, whose wife had lately died; and as she refused to go to his house, they hired a ruffian, for twelve shillings, to tie a rope around her and drag her there. Her boy, who had never before been separated from her by day nor night, clung to her screaming, but was torn away and kept in the family of his uncles.

One source of great unhappiness to Chinese women is in the law which forbids the breaking of betrothal contracts, even though these be made in the infancy of the parties involved. At one of the chapels somewhat remote from Swatow, a beautiful girl nineteen years old fled from her home to me and begged me to adopt her as my daughter. She said she would serve me as a slave if I would but steal her and carry her away concealed in my boat. She had been betrothed in childhood to a boy who had since developed a loathsome and incurable disease; and though she had not seen him, she knew how horrible he was, and would die rather than marry him. Her parents were not willing to carry out the contract they had made many years previously, but the boy's parents would not release them from the bargain. Her mother urged her to kill herself, as the only solution of the question. I sent agents to negotiate with the boy's parents, but could make no terms with them; and I also sought the officials and learned that they would not condone the withholding of a bride from even such a bridegroom. There was no legal way in which this child could be saved from her fate. Some weeks later she was taken to the house of her husband's parents, and soon after I heard of her death. Whether she died of grief or by suicide, I do not know. Suicide is not uncommon among brides, nor among older women. Some years ago seven young women, at a village near Swatow, entered into a compact to drown themselves together. Three of them had been lately married, and after spending the customary four months at the houses of their fathers-in-law, had come to visit their own mothers. They had been playmates, and were neighbours, and so they spun and sewed together, and rejoiced in their reunion. Mutual confidences revealed mutual griefs. One was married to an opium-smoker, a yellow bundle of bones, vibrating between besotted sleep and sottish waking. One was wedded to a gambler, who spent his days and nights wasting the family substance. One had a mother-in-law so stern and cruel that life was torment to those under her authority. All three of the brides were miserable, and as they mingled their lamentations, their four unmarried friends and companions said to each other, "This is such sorrow as we must feel by-and-by. How much better to be dead!" All agreed in this, and entered secretly into a covenant to end their lives together.

They calculated the time when custom would again bring the married ones to their mothers' houses, and fixed the full moon of the seventh month, as the night for their escape from life. When the time arrived, six of them dressed themselves in festal garments, with flowers in their hair, went hand in hand in the moonlight to the shore, bound themselves together with a rope, and threw themselves into the sea. The seventh, only thirteen years old, was discovered through some noise she made in searching for her best clothing in the night, and was prevented by her mother from leaving the house. From her the fate of the other six was afterwards ascertained, and their bodies were recovered and buried in one grave. These are cases of extreme though not uncommon unhappiness, under the Chinese marriage-system.

CHAPTER II.

CHILD-LIFE IN CATHAY: THE STORY OF NUMBER FOUR.

ONCE upon a time, in the province of Kwang Tung, the department of Tie-Chiu, the district Kit-ie, and the village E Lim, lived a boy named A Si, which means Number Four. There were several boys of the same name in the village, and they were so called because they were fourth sons. The girls interspersed among them in the families counted for nothing. If you asked any of the people how many children they had, they only mentioned in reply the number of their sons, and said nothing about their daughters.

This village, E Lim, had about two thousand inhabitants, and lay near the foot of a range of mountains, from which the level rice-fields stretched away, dotted thickly with villages. All the people in it were of the same surname, and probably descended from one ancestor; though that ancestor lived so long ago that the people did not know whether they themselves were fifth or fiftieth cousins to each other. All the people in this village were named Heng; and one would need to be very familiar with the place in order to find any one he went to search for in it.

No matter where any inhabitant went to earn money, he always left his wife and children at home, with the ancestors who were dearer to him than his wife and children; and however far he might travel or however long he might be gone, he never lost the intention of coming back to this village before he died, and bringing with him all the money he might have. To him, home was home though ever so homely.

There was a strong stone wall around the village. The houses were all only one storey high, and the streets were so narrow that it was more convenient for two persons to walk in file than side by side. The pigs and chickens lived in the streets, before the door of the family to which they belonged, and went indoors at night.

In the centre of the village was an ancestral hall, toward the building of which all had contributed. It had carved and gilded flowers, crabs and tigers ornamenting the bare beams of the roof inside, porcelain flowers and birds on the ridgepole outside, and stone lions at the door. On one side were shelves full of little wooden tablets, with the names of ancestors thereon. At festivals, of which there are sixty-four in the Chinese year, people came and burned pieces of gilt paper, called spirit-money, and worshipped the tablets of their dead grandfathers and grandmothers.

On the outskirts of the village was a temple, as handsomely built as the ancestral hall, and containing, for the convenience of those who preferred one god to another, the images of several gods. To this temple came those who were going on a journey, those who had some business project in mind, those who wanted some especial thing, and those who feared some calamity, to worship and to make offerings of meats, cakes, and fruit to whichever god they thought had greatest influence on their particular case. They put the food on dishes in rows before the god, lighted incense-sticks to burn before him, and then got down on their hands and knees, and knocked their foreheads on the floor, explaining meanwhile their desires. Then they took away the meats offered to idols and ate them in their own houses.

The ancestral hall and the temple were the only public buildings of the place. Sometimes a shed was put up in front of the temple, as a theatrical stage. Several times a year the wealthy men of the village subscribed a sum equal to twelve or more pounds, sufficient to pay a company of actors to come there and play for three or more days and nights. The actors wore the costumes of ancient times, and had their garments of silk and crape embroidered with gold thread. They enacted the ancient history of China; and every one went to see them, though they spoke in the court language, which none of the common people understood. At the beginning of the play, the chief idol of the temple was carried in a decorated chair, followed by a long procession of actors and others dressed in uniform, round the village and to some of the neighbouring villages, and was then brought back to be the chief spectator at the succeeding performances. These theatres were the chief recreation of the people, and were attended by old and young. Many guests from other villages were entertained at that time, and many came to the play bringing their own provision of food for the day.

Back on the mountain were the graves of all who had been buried from this village for hundreds of years. The graves were dug horizontally into the hill, and before each was horseshoe-shaped masonry, three or four feet high in the centre, and sloping down to the ground at the ends. Seen from a distance, the burying-ground looked like a great city. Those of the Heng family who had died far outnumbered those who remained alive. During the second month of the Chinese year, all who had ancestors buried here came and fastened gilded paper to flutter over the grave, and worshipped before it. If any grave lacked for three years these offerings of paper, showing that it had not been visited by the descendants of the person buried in it, the land on which it was made could no longer be claimed as private property.

The people of E Lim were engaged chiefly in farming, getting three crops a year from their land. The women seldom went out of sight of their own houses, and were busy cooking, spinning, and weaving cotton and flax for the family garments.

When little Number Four was born in this village, his parents were very glad; for they thought that nobody could have too many sons. He was wrapped in a clean rag and laid in a basket, which hung by two cords over a beam in the roof, and in which he was swung to sleep. When he was one month old he had his head shaven in spots, and when he was four months old it was shaven clean. As it was cold weather, and there was never a fire in the house, he was kept warm by a little jacket thickly quilted with cotton, and by two old jackets of his father's wrapped around his legs. Long before he had teeth, his mother fed him with soft-boiled rice, which she deftly tucked into his mouth with her fingers, and on which he thrived wonderfully. When he fretted much, he was put into a pocket on the back of his eight-year-old sister, and she ran about or swayed to and fro to quiet him. Indeed, he spent the greater part of the first five years of his life on his mother's or his sister's back, sitting in a scarf tied over her shoulders, his arms around her neck, his legs dangling at her sides, and his head bobbing back, looking at the roof or the sky. When he was three years old, the hair on his crown was allowed to grow long to be braided into a queue. Almost as soon as he could walk and carry a basket and rake, he went with his next elder brother to gather fuel on the hills. They scraped up the dry wild grass and the fallen needles of the pine-trees, and everything else they could gather to make the pot boil. They had to supply all the fuel that was used for the family cooking, and rarely got beaten except when they failed to gather enough.

Number Four wore a bamboo hat, made in basket-work, lined with leaves, and as large as a parasol. The remainder of his costume was a short cotton jacket and very loose short cotton trousers. His skin was yellow, and his eyes and hair jet black.

When Number Four grew older he had another employment, that of leading the buffalo which his father owned, and which helped to work the land. This buffalo was larger than a common ox; its skin was like a pig's, and covered with coarse, sparse, mouse-coloured hair; and its horns were long, sharp, and curved. It dragged the plough and harrow over the rice-fields, and when at rest as well as when at work must have an attendant to lead it from place to place to feed, and to see that it did not destroy the grain; for there were no fences between the fields. It was governed by a rope tied to a ring through its nostril. Number Four liked to ride home from the rice-field on its back, and then watch it while it rested and wallowed in a pool of muddy water. When there was not enough rain, Four had also to help to turn the chain pump, which raised water from the creek to the level of the rice-fields, to water the growing crop. This pump was turned by the feet, three persons stepping together on the flanges of a wheel, which turned the endless chain that brought up the water.

With all these occupations he had no time to go to school, though there were private schools in the village, where he might have had instruction by paying a tuition-fee of eight or ten shillings a year. His education was that which most effectively moulds the mind; it lay in the opinions and the practices of those around him. He was never taught not to lie, but he was certainly punished if he stole, and so he learned to respect the rights of property. He constantly heard maxims from the ancient sages, and proverbs in which the wisdom of generations was concentrated. He was taught worldly caution by, "Don't lace your boot in a melon-field, nor adjust your hat under a plum-tree"; reticence in speech by, "Diseases enter by the mouth, misfortunes issue from it," and "A coach-and-four cannot bring back a word once uttered"; modesty of behaviour by, "Who lifts his feet high has put on boots for the first time"; contentment by, "All ten fingers can't be of the same length"; mutual dependence by, "There is no peace for the mouth when one tooth is aching"; and for morality, he had the silver rule of Confucius, "Do nothing to others which you would not have others do unto you." In the densely crowded quarters where he lived, in his varied and numerous social relationships, and in the distinct duties enforced upon him, he learned self-control, patience, and diligence to an extent seldom attained by boys of other lands.

Besides attending the theatre, and going through the

religious ceremonies, Four did not often play, except in November when he flew a kite. The kites used were a paper star, fish, or bird, brilliantly painted; and the boys would send them up to fight with each other aloft. Some of them had a little wheel attached, and this, when turned by the wind, hummed as it went. Sometimes the boys fastened the strings of their kites, and left them humming all night, high in the air.

When Four was ten years old, his father died. On the seventh day thereafter, the sons bought paper clothing, trunks, and paper money, images of all the articles which he was supposed to require in the spirit-world, and burned them for his benefit. Not long after, an uncle also died, and they took the opportunity to send their father an additional quantity of clothing, burning it with their uncle's outfit.

As Four's mother was still young, they did not keep the father's coffin in the house till she died and could be buried with him, but carried it at once to the hills. A long procession followed it, the mourners being dressed in sack-cloth, with white threads braided in their hair. A hired band of musicians, blowing horns, preceded the coffin; and beans, peas, and grain were thrown into the grave, before the coffin was lowered. The place for the grave, and the day for the funeral, had been previously selected by a wizard, who was supposed to be able to discover what was lucky in such matters.

Shortly after this, a great man, from whom the father had borrowed money, came and demanded immediate payment. The family were in great distress, not having the means to pay the debt without selling the land on which their support depended. After much trouble, and many threats from the creditor, the mother decided to accept the offer of a rich relative to whom she had applied for help, and for a sum amounting to nearly twenty pounds let him have Number Four for his own son. Four and his mother and brothers all cried over it; but on what was found to be a fortunate day by casting lots in the temple, he went away, to be his mother's child no more. Papers of legal sale were made out, and his mother and brothers bound themselves never to make any claims of relationship upon him. Even if they became rich, they could never offer to buy him back again. His elder sister had been married long before, and the betrothal money spent. His younger sister was then betrothed for two pounds, and went at once to be brought up by the mother of her future husband. So the money due to the hard creditor was made up, and the mother had three boys left to support her in old age.

A Si, in his new home, was no longer Number Four. His name was changed to Kai Bun, which means "an aspirant in literature"; and his estate was so much improved, that it was only at times that he remembered his former home with regret. He here had one elder brother, who was also an adopted child; for this couple had no children of their own, and they must have some one to rear up as theirs, to make offerings for their welfare in the spirit-world after their death. Before this, Four had eaten boiled sweet-potatoes three times a day; but now he had rice, with fish, vegetables, pork, and poultry. He wore shoes with wooden soles an inch thick, and nankeen stockings, with his trousers tucked in at the top, and fastened there by bright blue silk garters. His jacket was now long and fine, and he wore a black satin cap. He also began to go to school. In reading, he began at what you would call the back of the book, and read down the columns of letters, beginning at the upper right-hand corner of the page, and ending at the lower left-hand corner. His teacher first read a few columns to him, and Kai Bun repeated these after him. Then he went to his seat and studied aloud at the top of his voice, as all the other boys did, until he had learned the lesson. Then he went and turned his back toward his teacher and repeated his lesson from memory. In this way he went over the whole book. When he was older, the meaning would be explained to him. He learned also to write, beginning by putting his copy under thin paper, and following it with a little brush wet with ink. After he had learned to hold his brush and guide his hand well, he wrote the copy from memory. Reading and writing would be his only studies, no matter how many years he remained at school.

When Kai Bun was fourteen, he for the first time saw a foreign lady in his village. Some of the children screamed and hid when they saw her; but a great many more followed her to the house where she sat down, and gazed at her with wide-open eyes, while she talked and answered questions. She had blue eyes and brown hair, and looked very strange to them. Some of them asked her if she was born with blue eyes, or whether her eyes had faded out; some asked her if she could see at all; and others asked if with such eyes she could see through a wall. Some asked if all the people in the country she came from had red hair; and some, if she painted her hands, as well as her face, to make them white. Some wanted to know if there were rice and potatoes and trees in her country; and some inquired whether her country was farther off than the one where all the inhabitants were women, and if it were really true that there were countries and people at the bottom of the sea. Another, who had heard of Great Britain, remarked that in Western lands they had women for their rulers. She had some books with her, and as Kai Bun could read, she lent him one, promising to make him a present of another when he should have read the first all through.

CHAPTER III.

THE EXTENT OF A GREAT CRIME.

IF we would truly help people, we must know their real need. Not till we comprehend their mode of thought, understand their peculiar temptations, gauge the pressure upon them of their surroundings, and apprehend their actual sorrows and sins, can we guide, console, or strengthen them. We must know just where the wound is if we would apply aright the balm.

In endeavouring to form for their good an intimate acquaintance with Chinese women, I came upon a fearful fact in their lives. Heathen women, with no flush of shame, no sense of guilt, mentioned to me in casual conversation that they had killed several of their own children. Christian women, with consciences quickened by the gospel, have come to me in tears, asking me to pray that this crime in their past lives might be blotted out from God's book of remembrance. In my journeys through the country, I frequently saw the bodies of dead infants, and was told that they were thrown away when living, because their parents did not want them. Wishing to know to what extent infanticide was practised, and what was the comparative rate of mortality among children of the two sexes, I wrote to several ladies in other parts of China, asking them to assist me in collecting statistics upon these points. I am indebted to their careful investigations and reliable replies for the information I possess concerning parts of China other than Swatow.

At Chefoo, of twenty-five aged mothers, none confessed to having destroyed any children; but none among them had reared more than three girls, and only two of them had reared more than two girls. At Tung Cho, near Peking, of twenty-five mothers, four had destroyed seven daughters. The resident missionary lady who inquired into this subject says :—

"Among our personal acquaintances there are few whose testimony I should rely on, on account of their fearing to be questioned, and of their superstition that having their names written may bring bad luck. These statistics have been obtained from our church-members principally, and are concerning themselves or their near acquaintances. They could not be used as representing the percentage of infanticide in this region. To say that four women in twenty-five destroy their female offspring would be untrue. I do not believe that one in a hundred does so, counting all classes, even the beggars. The crime is known : compared with the same in Christian lands, it is frequent. Heathenism is selfish and cruel everywhere, and so long as women lead the wholly dependent lives to which they are condemned in China, there will be many whose poverty, or whose desire for male posterity, will lead them to consider a daughter a burden rather than a comfort, and who in their hour of bitter disappointment will murder the child. As such a crime is never punished by the civil authorities here, the helpless little ones are wholly at the mercy of their mothers' impulses. But though we do occasionally hear of such cases, the crime, as a great and widespread evil, does not exist here."

At Kalgan, of seven mothers whose circumstances were known, five had destroyed no children, one had

The Extent of a Great Crime.

destroyed four, and one had destroyed two. At Hankow, of twenty-five women, eight had been guilty of infanticide, and had among them destroyed eighteen daughters. At Ningpo, I was told that infanticide is in later times seldom practised. In earlier days it was a common thing, but the government authorities stopped it when they found that wives were becoming scarce. Since then, associations have been formed who make it their business to provide for destitute girls, paying their parents a certain sum for caring for them up to a marriageable age. Some poor families sell their girls while yet a few years old, and the buyer trains them and sells them again for inferior wives. There are two or three districts in this region where infanticide used to be very common. From one of these came a blind woman, who is now a useful Christian. She lost her sight when about three years of age; and she thinks it must have been her step-mother, not her own mother, who, after she became blind, threw her into the canal once, twice, yea, thrice, hoping thus to put her out of the way. She each time felt her way up to the bank, and was helped out. The last time she was taken to her grandmother's to be cared for, and afterwards to an aunt's, going farther and farther from her original home till she reached Ningpo, at a distance of three or four hundred miles, where she lived by begging until taken up by the missionaries.

At Soochow, it is said that female infants are but rarely murdered. There are two very large and well-endowed foundling asylums in the city, and all mothers who do not want to bring up their daughters send them to an asylum. Ten or twelve children are often brought at a time from the country around Soochow, gathered up in baskets, and brought in like chickens. Both boys and girls are taken in at the asylums, and are farmed out to persons who offer to take care of them, and who are paid about four shillings a month for their trouble. When the children are old enough to be put to work, or to learn a trade, they are recalled by the Board of Managers, and provided with an occupation. Many poor men get their wives from among the foundlings, because they need pay but a small sum for them. Girls are also adopted into families, and are taken as servants; and afterwards husbands are procured for them. At one of these asylums, any woman too poor to provide clothing for her infant may apply for, and be supplied with, a complete baby outfit, and this mitigation of the expense encourages her to save her child alive.

In the Province of Fokien, the Governor has recently issued a proclamation forbidding infanticide, and meting out severe punishment to the offender. It is said that in some of the districts where this crime was formerly rife, it now scarcely exists. Newly-born female children readily bring from four to twelve shillings, and are sold to men who make a business of peddling babies. Twenty-one mothers in Foochow and its vicinity, whose domestic history was ascertained, had murdered, sold, or given away forty-six daughters. One remarkable case was found in which a mother reared six daughters; and the reason she gave for the singular fact was that her husband worked at a distance, and was never at home when the girls were born, and though he was very angry when he found their lives had been spared, he let them live because the mother loved them.

In the city of Amoy there is a foundling hospital, and infanticide is said to be much less common than in the adjoining country. Of twenty-five mothers at Amoy,

The Extent of a Great Crime. 23

none had reared more than two daughters; and five had destroyed eleven at their birth, while thirteen had been sold or given away. At Canton, where there are also native foundling hospitals, fifteen women had destroyed thirteen girls.

A Roman-Catholic priest, who had lived twenty-one years in Peking, told me that during the year 1882, seven hundred little castaway girls had been gathered up alive from the ruts and pits of the street, and brought in by the messengers sent out on such service from the Roman-Catholic foundling asylum of that city; and that during the previous ten years, over eight thousand infants had thus been found and sheltered by the same institution.

At Swatow, where I took accounts from forty women, each answering for herself alone, and each over fifty years of age, I found that the forty had among them destroyed seventy-eight of their daughters. The heathen women seldom allow more than two of their girls to live. The rearing of more than three is a marked exception to the rule. The decision whether any more girls are wanted is usually made in the family before the child's birth, and an undesired girl is stifled by the mother, father, or grandmother, as soon as her sex is known. A neighbour of one of my Bible-women bore six daughters successively, and smothered five of them. When the sixth came, she said it was always the same girl coming back, and she would no longer endure her. She wanted boys, and would see whether that girl could be deterred from again presenting herself. She cut the child into minute particles, and scattered them over the rice-fields.

The murder of other than newly-born infants is rare, but I know an instance in which the mother of a girl three months old died, and the father, finding the care and support of the child difficult, took it to the beach and left it till the tide washed it away to sea. That such a thing might be done in any land is credible. But that all the neighbours and relatives should know and acquiesce in such an act; that the man who did it should not lose social caste ; and that the drowning of a three-months'-old girl should excite no more comment than the drowning of a kitten, in a village of three thousand people, is marvellous to anyone who does not know how lightly the lives of Chinese girls are esteemed. I know of but two foundling hospitals within fifty miles of Swatow, but there may be others. At one of these, from one to two hundred infant girls are taken in during a year. They are at once given out to nurse, twopence a day being paid the woman who nurses one of them When twelve or more days old, they are, if strong and well, put into baskets and carried out by a man who receives tenpence a day for hawking them in the villages round. Any woman who wishes to do so, examines the hawker's baskets, selects a daughter-in-law from among the contents, and the hospital is relieved from further care of the child.

Walking one nightfall near Go Chan, I met a man carrying two large covered hampers at the ends of a pole over his shoulder. Wailing voices issued from the hampers, and I asked the man to let me look at his burden. He lifted the covers, and I found that his wares consisted of three young infants, lying on their backs, cold, hungry, and miserable. This baby-peddler had taken six little girls out that morning to sell. He had disposed of only half his stock, and was going home with the remainder. He said he was tired and had yet a long way to go, and

The Extent of a Great Crime. 25

that, if I would take the lot, I might have all three of the girls for four shillings.

In conversation with forty different women, each alone, and with no reason for telling me other than the truth, and all over fifty years of age, I learned that the forty women had borne a hundred and eighty-three sons and a hundred and seventy-five daughters. Of these sons, a hundred and twenty-six had lived to be more than ten years old; while only fifty-three of the daughters had reached that age. The question at once arises, whether there is not a large surplus male population in this region, and whether there are not many men unable to find wives. Nearly all the adult men are married, though the betrothal money averages eight pounds, and the expenses of a wedding are considerable. The population is so dense, that even though the land is divided into small fields, worked by their owners and yielding three crops a year, the maximum number that can live on its produce is far exceeded. The women do not go abroad, and the number of little girls allowed to live is regulated by the number that can be fed. The custom of binding their feet makes them the more useless, and therefore the more subject to murder. The men may emigrate, and by their earnings abroad help to support their parents. The forty women mentioned had sons abroad equal in number to the daughters they had destroyed, and a large proportion of these sons were sending money to their parents.

Combining the statistics gathered by missionary ladies in the above-mentioned places with those I have myself collected, I find that a hundred and sixty Chinese women, all over fifty years of age, had borne six hundred and thirty-one sons and five hundred and thirty-eight daughters. Of the sons, three hundred and sixty-six, or nearly sixty per cent., had lived more than ten years; while of the daughters, only two hundred and five, or thirty-eight per cent., had lived ten years. The hundred and sixty women had, according to their own statements, destroyed a hundred and fifty-eight of their daughters; but none had ever destroyed a boy. As only four of these women had reared more than three girls, the probability is that the number of infanticides confessed to is considerably below the truth. I have occasionally been told by a woman, that she had forgotten just how many girls she had had more than she wanted. The greatest number of infanticides owned to by any one woman was eleven.

The causes of this crime are two, poverty and superstition. The acceptance of Christianity brings about a cessation of child-murder, because it destroys the superstition which is its cause, leading the parents to depend on God, not on male descendants, for comfort in the life to come. It does not obviate the poverty, but it presents life in a new aspect, as an opportunity for acquiring moral and spiritual perfection; and for this the saddest life often furnishes the best opportunity.

CHAPTER IV.

FOOT-BINDING.

THE process of binding, the style of shoe worn, and the social condition of the victim, vary considerably in different parts of the empire. The rich bind the feet of their daughters at six or eight years; the poor, at thirteen or fourteen. They are seldom bound later than at fifteen; though a case is known in which poor parents, who had sold their daughter as a slave, became rich, reclaimed her, and bound her feet when she was twenty years old.

The appliances for binding include no iron nor wooden shoe. Only long strips of firm, flexible cloth are used. We are often asked to admire the moulding power of soft influences: perhaps we too seldom consider that they are as powerful for evil as for good. I once saw a sturdy tree inwreathed and clasped to death by a fragile vine.

The bandages used in mis-shaping the feet are woven in small hand-looms, and are about two inches wide and ten feet long. One end of the bandage is laid on the inside of the instep; thence it is carried over the four small toes, drawing them down upon the sole; then it passes under the foot, over the instep, and around the heel, drawing the heel and toe nearer together, making a bulge on the instep, and a deep niche in the sole underneath; thence it follows its former course until the bandage is all applied, and the last end is sewn down firmly on the underlying cloth. Once a month or oftener, the feet, with the bandages upon them, are put into a bucket of hot water and soaked. Then the bandages are removed, the dead skin is rubbed off, the foot is kneaded more fully into the desired shape, pulverized alum is laid on, and clean bandages quickly applied. If the bandages are long left off, the blood would again circulate in the feet, and the rebinding would be very painful. The pain is least when the feet are so firmly and so constantly bound as to be benumbed by the pressure of the bandages.

It not infrequently happens that the flesh becomes putrescent during the process of binding, and portions slough off from the sole. Sometimes a toe or more drop off. In this case the feet are much smaller than they could else be made, and elegance is secured at the cost of months of suffering. The pain ordinarily continues about a year, then gradually diminishes, till at the end of two years the feet are practically dead and painless.

During this time the victim of fashion sleeps only on her back, lying across the bed, with her feet dangling over the side, so that the edge of the bedstead presses on the nerves behind the knees in such a way as to dull the pain somewhat. There she swings her feet and moans, and even in the coldest weather she cannot wrap herself in a coverlet, because every return of warmth to her limbs increases the aching. The sensation is said to be like that of having the joints punctured with needles.

While the feet are being formed they are useless, and their owner moves about the room to which she is confined, by putting her knees on two stools, so that her feet will not touch the floor, and throwing her weight upon one knee at a time, while she moves the stools alternately forward with her hands.

When the feet are completely remodelled, there is a notch in the middle of the sole deep enough to conceal a pennypiece put in edge-wise across the foot. The four small toes are so twisted that their ends may be seen on the inside of the foot; and the broken and distorted bones of the middle of the foot are pressed into a mass where the instep should be. The shape is like a hen's head, the big toe representing the bill. There is little beside skin and bone below the knee. The foot cannot be stood on without its bandages, and can never be restored to its natural shape. It is a frightful and fetid thing. No bound-footed woman ever willingly lets her bare feet be seen, even by those who are maimed like herself. She wears little cotton shoes when in bed, putting as it were her night-cap on her feet.

The sepulchre for these mummied feet is very gorgeous. The bandages and alum-powder are always worn; but the bandages are shortened one-half their length, and fine black ones are often put on over the white ones. Embroidered satin shoes, with brightly painted heels, are worn, and a neat pantalet covers all but the toe. What is visible appears to be the petal of a field-lily.

Even outside barbarians often admire this fairy foot. Yet the poet cannot say of the owner,

"Her foot so light, her step so true,
  Scarce from the harebell brushed the dew."

Her dainty feet toddle and clump, and her gait is exactly that of one walking on the points of the heels.

Though the Chinese poet compares her motion to that of the swaying willow, one never sees among Chinese women one who walks gracefully. Those who have natural feet imitate the vacillating hobble of the bound-footed, verifying the Italian proverb, "If you always live with those who are lame, you will yourself learn to limp."

In walking, the small-footed lean on a child's shoulder or use a supporting staff. Those who can afford it, have large-footed female slaves who carry them about on their backs, for short distances. I have been to visit a wealthy family and had the neighbouring ladies come in to see me, each riding pick-a-back on her slave. A lady, whose beautiful house I went to see, was as gracious a hostess as could be found in any land; but her feet were so tiny that the longest walk she could take was from one room to the next, and she was obliged to sit down after walking a few steps on her marble floors. I have seen those whose feet were but two inches long upon the sole, and their shoes were no larger than those of a young infant. Only the very rich can afford to be so helpless as such feet render their possessor, and there are not many who are very rich.

Middle-class women, with bound feet, sometimes walk four or five miles in a day. Many whose feet are apparently bound have natural shaped feet, merely dressed in the style of the bound-footed. In some villages, the girls have their feet slightly bound just before marriage, and unbind them soon after the wedding festivities are past. In some hamlets the women are all large-footed, and wade streams and walk long distances bare-footed; but on approaching a town, and on gala days, they do up their feet, more or less successfully, in the aristocratic style.

Foot-Binding. 31

The Hakka women do not bind their feet ; they lead a vigorous physical life, working chiefly in the open air. The better custom of these people influences those living on their borders, and the country women in their vicinity do not bind their feet. On their side of Tie Chiu, among those who live in hamlets and small villages, the custom is slowly dying out. In one cluster of hamlets where twenty years ago every girl's feet were bound, no one now binds a daughter's feet. This laxity is unfortunately confined to the country villages in the neighbourhood of the Hakkas. In the cities and large towns, all women, except slaves and bond-servants, have deformed feet.

Foot-binding is not so much a matter of class as of locality. Near the coast, even in the farmsteads and among the most indigent, every woman has bound feet. It is not a voucher for respectability, for the vilest are often bound-footed. Neither is it a sign of wealth, for in those places where the custom prevails, the poorest follow it. Inferior wives, unless they come as bond-maids into the household, are usually bound-footed women. Taking all China together, probably nine-tenths of the women have bound feet.

The evils that accrue from this custom are very great. It makes cripples of nearly half the population, and adds immensely to the misery of the poverty-stricken multitudes. It disables women from supporting themselves and from caring for their children, and is one of the causes of the great prevalence of infanticide. It renders women too weak to keep their houses clean, and makes their homes filthy and cheerless. It incapacitates woman for travelling, and keeps her and her thoughts in the narrowest of spheres. Why any should follow so pernicious a practice is one of the mysteries of human perversity. There is no law that women shall bind their feet, and the women of the imperial palace at Peking are all natural-footed. The origin of the custom is unknown lost in the mists of antiquity.

The only reason that I have heard in favour of it, aside from the common one that women would be laughed at and despised if their feet were like men's, was given me by a man, who said that it was necessary that women's feet should be bound, else they would be as strong as their husbands, and then they could not be kept in subjection by beating.

But the men generally offer no greater opposition to a departure from the established fashion than do the women themselves. For a Chinese woman the greatest of sorrows is that of having no sons: the next to the greatest is that of being unlike her neighbours. The smallest feet are made by those who determine to be elegant at any cost, and these draw their own foot-ligatures tighter than any one else would draw them. Religion is not the only sentiment which has its martyrs.

CHAPTER V.

AN ESPOUSAL.

THE Chinese say that a woman marries, while a man takes a wife. Being at Kui-Su, a town forty miles west of Swatow, where no foreign lady had ever before been, I was so fortunate as to make the acquaintance of the ladies of one of the families in the place, and was invited by them to a wedding. As a foreigner seldom has the opportunity to see a purely pagan family throughout a domestic festivity like this, I was glad to accept the invitation.

[During the previous evening there was a puppet-show, costing eight shillings, on a little stage before the door of the house of the bridegroom's father. It was, like all Chinese theatrical performances, free to all who chose to come and look, being called and paid for by the host. Indoors, racks on two sides of the main room were filled with baskets holding cakes, which the family and its relatives had for many days been employed in making. A red silk curtain was suspended against the wall opposite the chief door, while scrolls having congratulatory sentences written upon them, the gifts of invited guests, were hung thickly on the side walls. A table in the centre of the room was piled tastefully with cakes and confectionery. A band of music played all the evening, and all passers-by went in to see the festive arrangements. Early in the morning the bride was brought home in a sedan-chair covered with scarlet cloth. She was sixteen years old, an only daughter, and had been betrothed for five years. The engagement was made by a woman, called a go-between, whose business was match-making; and neither the bride nor her parents had ever seen the bridegroom. Her parents had received nearly six pounds for her, from the bridegroom's father, and were to receive eight shillings more in money, and three pounds' worth of food, on the following day. She had the evening before been washed in water with twelve kinds of flowers in it; and she was dressed in red silk trousers, a green silk petticoat, and a blue silk tunic. Over these was a scarlet robe, extending from neck to feet. Her hair was almost concealed by gilt ornaments, and she wore a veil of red gauze, under another of red silk fringe. I was told that her duty was to cry aloud on leaving home, else she failed in respect to her parents. She was accompanied from home only by the go-between and another old woman, the mistress of ceremonies; and she would see none of her own relatives for four months, after which time she would return for a visit to her parents. On her arrival at her father-in-law's house, she was taken into a small room, where she stayed till she was brought out and placed beside her husband at the wedding breakfast. At this only the bride and groom sat down, and only the groom ate. The groom was an only son, seventeen years old; and his father was considered a man of means, having some four hundred pounds invested in his business. He wore green trousers, a brown tunic, and a black hat with a red tassel on the top. During the meal the bride sat with her hands folded, and her head bowed behind her veil; and the mistress of ceremonies stood beside the bridegroom and with a pair of long chopsticks picked tidbits for him from the numerous dishes on the table. With each thing she took up in her chopsticks, she chanted a stanza of four lines. She predicted that the next year they would welcome a male child; that they would have seven sons and three daughters; that their daughters would all be handsome, and that their sons would take literary degrees; that they would build new houses, and would be wealthy, and would live long. After the bridegroom had made an abundant breakfast, in which he manifested great liking for lobster, the bride returned to her room, and the bridegroom was called to untie the inner veil, which was then taken off her face, and she peered out through the red silk fringe. Then she was placed on a chair at the foot of her red bridal-couch, with piles of red boxes, containing her wardrobe, on either side of her; and there she remained all day, silent and motionless.

Meanwhile, all the family and kin were engaged in preparations for the evening feast. About dark, messengers were sent to call each of the invited guests, who were all men. I sat behind a screen at the door of a side-room where the women were, and looked on. In the main room, five red tables, each three feet square, were ranged at comfortable distances apart, with seats for two on each side. A tiny wine-cup, a pair of chopsticks, an earthen spoon, and a small saucer, were placed for each guest. A dish of sweetmeats was at each corner of the table, and two decanters for hot wine were at one side. The host, the bridegroom's father, stood near the door, facing it; and each guest, as he arrived, stood in the door while the host went and relaid the chopsticks, slightly moved the chair, and made a low obeisance before the place which this guest was to occupy. The guest thén went and stood at the seat indicated by the host. When the chief guests, two at each table, had thus been placed, those of lesser importance came in, the host pointed out their seats without ceremony, and all sat down simultaneously. All guests wore tunics reaching to their feet, and red tasselled hats. The host did not sit down at supper, but superintended the bringing of food for the guests. When he himself placed a dish on a table, all the guests at that table rose to receive it. The servants brought the food on trays, and placed a bowlful in the centre of each table, and all ate from the common dish, deftly picking up the lumps of food with their two chopsticks, held as we hold a pen, in the right hand. All the food was in lumps or slices, requiring no use of knives, and being perfectly prepared for chopstick manipulation. Some of it swam in broth which was eaten with a porcelain spoon. Two at table frequently poured hot wine into the cups of all. There were thirty-two dishes, each of such mixed ingredients as to form a complete course in itself, and the dishes increased in size toward the end of the feast. Among the dishes which I recognised, were chicken, salt duck, fish, pork boiled in molasses, bean-curd, chestnuts sliced and boiled in sweet soup, and olives. All was minced and mixed, and there was nothing on the bill-of-fare to which a French cook would affix *au naturel*. I noticed an economical device in the large dishes, that of laying a huge turnip in the middle, so that the apparently heaped-up delicacies had a kernel of less cost. There was no conversation during the meal, and no greater hilarity than frequent bows and infrequent monosyllables. Each gave his grave attention to the business in hand, and ate "without haste and without rest." The bride-

An Espousal. 37

groom, fearing practical jokes after supper, left the room about the middle of the feast, and was seen no more that evening. A band of four musicians, hired for about twelve shillings, played during the supper. Toward the end, the mistress of ceremonies went to each table in turn, chanted a stanza in honour of the guests thereat, and placed on the table a tray with eight cups of tea. Each guest drank the tea, replaced the cup, and dropped into it from twenty to a hundred cash (from one to five pence), which was removed to be divided between the go-between and the mistress of ceremonies. At the end of the feast, indicated by the bringing on of pellets of dough, all rose and went to another apartment. Then the women and children poured out from the side-rooms and quickly arranged the tables for their own supper, setting out all that was left from the masculine repast. When the women had supped, the tables were cleared away, the women returned to the side-rooms, and the male guests, who were not relatives, returned to see the bride. She did not appear in the large room, but with the go-between supporting her on one side and the mistress of ceremonies on the other, she approached the door of the small room in which she had been all the evening sitting, and the male guests came to the door, with candles in their hands, to look at her. The festivity seemed to consist in urging her to come one step nearer, and in asking to see her small feet. She looked steadily at the floor, silent, and with unchanging face, and only moved forward when lifted along by the two old women. When they raised her veil for a moment, she threw her long sleeves over her face; whereupon the old women withdrew her into a dark corner of the room, and the guests returned to their laboured merriment in the large room. This exhibition of the bride was repeated several times, the impudence of the guests increasing until, in any enlightened land, it would have brought the fists of the bride's father or brother in their faces. When my wrath had reached such a pitch that I was about to undertake, in the bride's behalf, the duties of a brother, and rise up to slay those sixteen Chinamen, they threw some handfuls of cash on the table as "a reward for seeing her face," and went home. I asked a woman who sat beside me if she did not think it was a shameful thing for the bride to be so treated, and she answered that such was Chinese custom, and inquired if they did not do so in my country. The bride slept in her new red bed, her bridal chamber being a corner of the family kitchen.

The next morning, the bride and groom worshipped the ancestral tablets and paid obeisance to the older members of the family. Red chairs covered with red cloth were placed, one on each side of a table on which candles and incense were burning, and the newly married couple knelt before these three times, bowing their heads to the earth. The chair was slightly moved, and the cloth rearranged, as each new person was thus emblematically worshipped. Some of those worshipped were absent. Those present rose from their seats, in any part of the room, and stood while they were being worshipped impersonally at the red chair. Then the bride gathered up the skirt of her red tunic, to hold the gifts of money that were put into it by those to whom she had done homage, and each put in a few small or one larger silver coin. This would be used by the father-in-law in defraying the expenses of the wedding. After this the bride retired to her bedroom, and her

An Espousal. 39

head-ornaments and red dress were removed. Then all the household beside prepared to send off the presents of food to the bride's family. Three hundred and sixty little red mince-pies, forty red puffs of rice-flour, two cakes three feet across, lobsters, pork, fish, fowls, and confectionery, were put in red boxes, and carried on the shoulders of bearers to their house, three miles away. Then the important ceremonies of the wedding were over.

As it would be considered very unlucky for the bride to see a person dressed in mourning, or one who had lately borne a child, or to eat anything from a house where there had recently been a death or a marriage, she would be carefully looked after during the succeeding four months. Then she would visit her parents, and after that she would begin her life-work of serving the elder members of her husband's family. She would rear chickens and pigs, cook, wash, carry burdens, and hope for male children as her chief good. There are lands in which women who have lost the highest social joy turn sadly and find consolation in the affection of their children. Here the sweetest love a woman dreams of is that of her little ones, and even her maternal love is degraded because she has known no other. There is no romance in the life of a Chinese woman, and nothing chivalrous in the character of a Chinese man. Here is a nation which has had four thousand years in which to prove what unassisted humanity can do for itself: and its women have no higher joy than the certainty that they shall always have enough to eat, and its men no nobler ambition than to have numerous descendants.

CHAPTER VI.

THE INVISIBLE BRIDEGROOM.

AN old woman told me this story, referring to one of her own relatives. We were discussing the evils which arise from the custom of betrothing young children to each other. Such engagements, made by the parents, without the knowledge of the young people, are no less binding than the marriage itself. They cannot indeed be legally broken, and seldom fail of being fulfilled. It is far more common for a husband to sell his wife than for a girl to be set free from the pledges her parents have made for her. The only recourse left to a girl who is married to a hated husband is to commit suicide, or to behave so badly that she will be sold to some other man.

A rich man had a chief wife and several inferior wives. The first wife had but one son, while the subordinate wives had several. One day a wealthy man, from a town a day's journey away, came on business, and sat conversing with this gentleman in his study, while the chief wife's son, then a bright, active boy four years old, played about the room. The beauty and activity of the boy attracted the attention of the visitor, and he mentioned that he himself had a daughter of the same age. An agreement was soon entered into, between the two fathers, that the children should espouse each other; and a go-between was employed, horoscopes cast, and all

The Invisible Bridegroom. 41

the rites of a betrothal accomplished. There was no further intercourse between the two families for many years. The girl grew up, and was of lovely disposition, unusual beauty, and fine talents. She was skilled in needlework, and could read and write. When she was sixteen, her wedding-day came, and she was carried to her mother-in-law's house. Her mother had prepared her wedding outfit of five hundred garments, with much jewellery, and exquisite appliances for the occupations she loved; and her father-in-law spent two hundred pounds in fitting up her bridal chamber, and in the entertainment of wedding guests.

Wealthy and cultured brides see little company, and after her arrival at her mother-in-law's house, she did not for months leave her own room. She spent her time in reading, embroidery, and painting; and was waited upon by four handmaidens, two of whom were given her by her own mother, and two by her mother-in-law. At the end of four months, she had neither seen nor heard of her husband. At this time it is customary for the mother of a bride to send a sedan chair, and invite her daughter to return and visit her parents; but this girl declined her mother's invitation, because she felt unable to answer the questions of her former associates about her present domestic life. She sent excuses to her mother, and was widely commended for her filial devotion to her mother-in-law. She could not so far depart from that modest reticence becoming a young woman as to make any inquiries in regard to her husband; and a year more passed without sign of him. Then, when she had pondered the matter much, she chose a time when only her handmaidens were with her, and asked one of them if she had ever seen her master.

The girl answered, "Certainly: I see him every day, and will lift him in for you to see if you wish it."—"Why must you lift him in? Can he not walk?"—"No, he cannot walk."—"Has he a sore foot?"—"No, he has not a sore foot."—"When do you see him?"—"When I go to feed him."—"Is he ill?"—"No, he is not ill." "Why does he not come here?"—Because we were told not to fetch him till you asked for him. Shall we bring him now?"—"Yes." So the handmaidens went and brought in a man in a large basket, and placed him beside their mistress's chair. He was full-grown, but utterly helpless, so that he could not move his limbs, and had never learned to talk. He wept when he saw the consternation of his wife, and seemed to try to comfort her with inarticulate sounds.

She sent for her father to come, and he looked on the rickety lad, and could not speak a word for sorrow. He took his daughter's pen, and wrote, "Daughter, it is your fate," and gave her the paper and turned away homeward without a word more.

This girl was so gently bred, and the two families were so respectable, that there was no thought of dissolving the marriage. Her family could not complain, for the boy was well when the betrothal was made, and began to grow helpless immediately afterward, showing that her star was a baleful one for him. There could be no recriminations from either side. The mother-in-law adopted four boys as sons for this girl, and hoped she would take some interest in life. But she pined continually, and died in three years. The cripple lived to be over thirty years old. His adopted sons lived, married, thrived, inherited the chief part of the estates, and now make offerings at the tombs of the ancestors.

CHAPTER VII.

HABITATIONS.

THOUGH the masses of the people are farmers, they live in villages, not in isolated houses; and the villages are so numerous all over the land that many others may be seen from any one of them. The people are the farthest possible from being nomadic. Generation after generation of the same family live in the same house and till the same fields, which descend surely from father to son.

Most people dwell in hovels, sleeping and eating, with their pigs and chickens, in a single room. Cholera prevails all summer, small-pox all winter, and vermin all through the year. They are densely crowded into their quarters, and few individuals have a separate room. I have only one Chinese acquaintance, who occupies alone a brown-stone front. A great brown rock has in some past age toppled over upon another rock in such a way as to form the roof and side of a sort of lean-to, and in the crevice underneath a bachelor makes his abode, and stores the tools he uses and the paddy he raises on the fields near by. He has built up with stones and mortar the two wide openings in the ends of his apartment, and he avoids the necessity for having a chimney by doing his cooking out of doors. The glinting of his fire often adds picturesqueness to the rugged hill-side of which he is the sole inhabitant. By far the greatest portion of the population live in huts, which are rendered hovels by the accumulations of filth in and around them. The walls are of some sort of cheap and rough mason-work. The roof is of tiles, upheld by beams and slats of pine. The only opening in the room is one door, and when this is closed, the light is admitted through two or three flakes of translucent shell or glass set in the roof. The floors are of earth, pounded hard and level. The furniture of these dwellings consists usually of pine beds and trestles, a deal table, earthen furnaces and pots, and piles of indescribable rubbish. As hardly any one lives, or would be willing to live, in an isolated house, these huts are built, with no interstices between them, along streets a yard wide, or round paved courts where clothes are dried, pigs reared, and food cured in the sun. A somewhat better dwelling-house is built with its door in a high wall on the street; behind this front door is a small court open to the sky, and containing perhaps a well, a few flowering shrubs in pots, and possibly some vines clambering up a trellis. On either side the court are rooms opening upon it, and at its inmost end is a large room used in common by all the inmates, and having on its wall, opposite the street-door, a grand shelf for the family gods. This common room is often the receptacle of the garnered produce of the land, and of the farming implements, and of the looms, dye-pots, and washtubs of the women of the household. Opening out of it on either side are two bedrooms, usually occupied by the older members of the family. When sons grow old, and wives are brought home for them, the rooms are apportioned so that each son shall have one; and several married brothers and their children often live with the parents, and perhaps with grandparents and uncles, in one house.

Habitations. 45

The great mass of the Chinese nation live thus in unventilated, unceiled, and unfloored rooms, that are terribly hot in summer, terribly cold in winter, and full of stench always. Probably nine hundred and ninety-nine thousandths of the population spend their lives in such unclean and uncomfortable homes.

The wealthy live in houses that are generally of but one storey, but they cover much ground, and are adorned with carving and painting. They include courts and gardens, with artificial grottoes, fish-pools, and lotus-ponds, all within a few yards of space. Epitomes of nature are greatly admired by the Chinese. The plastered walls are comparatively lofty, and are ornamented with pictures of birds, flowers, and historic scenes, or with curious scrolls. The roof-beams are carved, and the floors are laid in coloured tiles. The wide doors and many courts give light and air, and the impervious wall presented everywhere on the outer side, gives protection from thieves. These houses are furnished with articles in ebony and stone, carved in the highest style of Oriental art. Exquisite porcelain, bronze, jade, and silver vessels serve the occupants, who are clad in robes of embroidered satin and crape.

Though the Chinese style of house-building seems to us uncheerful, it is doubtless the one by which the inmate gets the greatest amount of comfort from the smallest amount of money. The wall without aperture discourages thieves, though the roof is vulnerable, making it necessary for someone to stay always in the house to guard against the goods being hooked up through a hole made by removing the tiles overhead. A ceiling would favour the dark dampness dear to white ants, and secure the rapid destruction of the roof-beams. The cheapest floor is that carried on their feet, in the thick wooden soles of their shoes. Wadded tunics are far less costly than fuel, and the expense of fireplaces and stoves is not incurred. Their loose, strong, and healthful garments, worn as well by night and in rest, as by day and at work, and their hardy habit of sleeping on a smooth board with only a straw mat over it, render narrow quarters endurable.

The real discomfort of their homes is due not so much to poverty as to superstition. The binding of the feet of the women disables them from much house-cleaning. The idea that white is an unlucky colour prevents whitewashing, and the walls become leprous. Their notions of geomancy hinder and bind them at every point. When, and not until, Christian truth shall have permeated the foundations of Chinese society, will the Chinese become well housed. Then, with no more money, the hovels may be cottages, and the huts homes.

The cities present a very uniform appearance, the houses being nearly all one storey in height, with the roofs nearly on a level, and covered with grey tiles. The cities are always walled, the walls being from fifteen to sixty feet in height, with strong gates, which are closed at nightfall. There are as many as seventeen hundred district and provincial cities, seats of local government. The provincial cities contain an average of one million inhabitants, and the district cities a hundred thousand.

CHAPTER VIII.

THE INCONVENIENCE OF HEATHENISM.

BESIDES the grave spiritual losses which accrue to the worshipper of false gods, there are constant earthly discomforts which come to him through his religion.

Whitewash is a well-known preparation, very cheap, and easily obtained. If applied to the walls of the hovels in which the masses of the people live, it would help to extirpate the vermin, and make the dreary rooms lighter and healthier. But white is an unlucky colour, and so buildings remain uncleansed for scores of years, their walls black with smoke, mould, and grime. I rented a small room opening into a chapel, at one of our stations, and desiring to use it as a bedroom for myself, asked the owner's permission to whitewash it. He begged me to abandon the project, because white was the colour worn in mourning, and to whitewash a room belonging to him would probably cause a death in his family. So I had to sleep, when at that station, in a room whose windowless walls were coated with the exhalations of several generations of occupants.

Rooms are often destitute of light and ventilation, because windows are supposed to afford egress to evil spirits which may injure the occupants of neighbouring houses. I have several times proposed cutting windows in the walls of rented houses at country stations, and have been told that some neighbour strenuously objected to my so doing, because of the fatal effects to him which might follow. Fortunately, however, there are cases in which an earthen tiger with open mouth, or even a pot or basket, placed on the roof of the dwelling opposite, catches the evil emanations, and makes the window harmless to humanity.

All the roads are so intricate and tortuous that none but an old resident attempts to travel, even from one village to the next, without a guide. To direct one to a place in any other way than by leading him is difficult. Of necessity, all parties of travellers are "personally conducted." In visiting among our church members, and in teaching in the hamlets, I at first pondered much upon the fact that the Chinese did not appear to have discovered that a straight line is the shortest distance between two points. I would start for a village that looked as if it were but a short distance away on the plain, but the road to it was always many times farther to my feet than to my eye. After awhile I learned that all roads and canals are made labyrinthian, so that wandering evil spirits may not easily find their way to the abodes of the inhabitants of the land.

A city of two hundred thousand persons has beside its walls a tidal canal, through which hundreds of boats pass monthly. But the canals are so shallow at the bridges when the tide is out, that boats must unload in order to pass; while, on the other hand, the bridges are so low that when the tide is high boats must be sunk deeper in the water by laying in heavy cargo, in order to get under the bridge. The result is that at times the

The Inconvenience of Heathenism. 49

boats are so packed in the canal as to make it impassable, and at all times the traffic of a great city is impeded, and almost ruined, by eight low bridges. These cannot be raised, because high structures, other than those devoted to the gods, are supposed to have a deleterious influence upon surrounding dwellings.

As the prosperity of a household is supposed to depend on having the graves of its dead progenitors in such sites as are satisfactory to their occupants, no parent is buried until a soothsayer has selected a spot for the tomb. The rules governing the choice of burial-places are occult, and it is often difficult to find among the hills the exact conformation of land and the precise relations to wind and water constituting a favourable locality for a grave. Therefore the encoffined dead are frequently kept in the habitations of the living, for many years, to the detriment of the whole surviving family.

Great and useless expense attends the observance of geomantic rules. In Soochow, twin pagodas were built in the form of Chinese pens, and for some time thereafter the scholars of the quarter of the city in which these pagodas stood were very successful in the examinations, and an unusual number took literary degrees, while the scholars in other parts of the city were unsuccessful. The lucky candidates were much complained of for having, through the pen-pagodas, drawn to themselves the good luck which ought to be equally distributed over the town, and a remedy was sought and adopted by the wronged scholars. They built in their own district another pagoda, representing an immense cake of ink, and thereafter shared the benefits bestowed by the gods on those who revere writing materials.

People so poor that they lack sufficient food, spend hard-earned money on offerings made to gods and demons, and even then fail to escape from dread and terror of these beings.

There came under my personal observation the following sad case. A couple had been married many years, and had no children. The wife made many prayers and offerings in a neighbouring temple, and promised the idol a splendid feast if she should have a son. At last her desire was fulfilled, and the delighted couple wished to pay their vow to the idol. But they were very poor, having only a bit of land from which they obtained their whole living. They considered much what they should do. They had no rich friends from whom to borrow, no handsome clothes that they could pawn, and no way of earning more than their daily bread; yet the idol must be satisfied, else it might do great harm to them and their child. There was only the land, which was their sole dependence. After much distressed debate, in which fear of the idol prevailed, they sold the land for six pounds, and spread a thanksgiving feast before the god. Then they struggled on, not hopelessly, because they had a son, and therefore need not be afraid that they would go naked and hungry in their old age in this world, nor in the world of spirits. By working at odd jobs here and there, they managed to keep themselves alive and to feed the child. When the boy was eight years old, another son was born to them. Again the idol must have a thank-offering; but this time they had no land to sell and were in the last stages of poverty. Their only valuable possession was their eight-year-old boy. He was bright and handsome, and a rich, childless man wanted him for his son. After much discussion, agitated by fear of the idol, and by desire for its beneficent influence on the babe, and all other means of getting money having failed, they sold the boy for three pounds, and again made a feast before the god. The elder boy gone, and the feast over, the baby took small-pox and died. The raving, despairing mother carried the corpse and bound it on the breast of the idol, saying, "You have eaten our house, you have eaten our pots and pans, you have eaten our eight-year-old boy: all we ever had has gone into your maw. Now eat this!"

The reckoning of times causes grave losses. The Chinese have, for over four thousand years, divided time into cycles of twelve and cycles of ten, five of the former and six of the latter making contemporaneously the great cycle of sixty. The numbers in the cycle of twelve are represented by twelve animals, the rat, the ox, the tiger, the hare, the dragon, the serpent, the horse, the goat, the ape, the cock, the dog, and the hog. The numbers in the cycle of ten are allotted to five substances, wood, fire, earth, metal, and water. Each year, month, day, and hour has thus a binary designation, and is reckoned as belonging to each of these two perpetually revolving cycles; and a time is lucky or unlucky according to the harmony or disagreement between the representatives of these four divisions of time. By consideration of these, horoscopes are cast, fortunate days chosen, and the most favourable moment for the transaction of important business decided upon. If the year belongs to water, and the day to fire, the time would be unlucky, unless its character were changed by some influence in the month and hour, which would obviate the danger arising from the collision of elements so inimical to each other as are fire and water. Since metals are melted by fire, these two, coming together in the cycle, would make the season unpropitious; while each might meet any of the other four elements without danger.

Then the animals in the cycle of twelve have enmities or affinities with each other and with the elements in the cycle of ten, and to calculate the results of their collision is a profound problem, supposed to have an immense influence in human affairs.

Blind men are the chief calculators of horoscopes. They learn their trade from more or less expert masters, and live upon their earnings. They go about the country on foot, leaning on the shoulder of a child guide, with a bag to hold their tools and gains, and a bell to announce their coming. When a Chinese mother has a new child, she generally calls in a blind fortune-teller to advise her concerning the peculiar dangers to which her offspring is exposed, and to tell her what offering she must make to the gods to induce them to protect it from harm. She gives the fortune-teller the necessary data, and he casts a horoscope founded on the numbers representing, in the two cycles, the year, month, day, and hour of the child's birth, and tells her what troubles she must forestall. She begs him to make offerings and to importune his god in behalf of her infant, and he mentions a sum which will suffice to cover the expense of these rites. She perhaps demurs at the cost. He then tells her that she may herself make the necessary offerings to some god in a neighbouring temple, and proceeds to give a list of the articles she must offer in order to preserve the child. As the list lengthens, she becomes frightened at the prospective outlay, and hastily agrees to pay him the sum he first mentioned as the price of taking all trouble off

The Inconvenience of Heathenism. 53

her hands. His charge is commonly from one to four shillings if the child be in good health and the woman poor. Though his demands be extortionate, the woman dare not dismiss him in anger, lest he use the data she has given him in making charms which will injure her child. The bargain completed, he gives her a little bag of incense to be worn by the child as an amulet, and then he goes on his way. The fortune-teller is not held responsible for the fate of the child; and probably the mother never saw him before, and will never see him thereafter. It is said that as many as eighty mothers in every hundred have a horoscope cast for their children when under a month old.

In the astrological almanack, the lucky days corresponding to all birthdays are given, and any one who can read can find them. For starting on a journey, for beginning to build any dwelling, for moving into a house, for opening new ground, for digging a well or a pit, for mending a roof, for making a kitchen range, for setting up a mill, for starting a web of cloth, for shaving a child's head the first time, for dressing a girl's hair in womanly style, for setting up a bride's bedstead, for bringing home a wife, for dividing the ancestral property, for putting a corpse in its coffin, for a funeral, and indeed for every enterprise, a lucky day must be found. Without this, some accident will happen, or some untoward event will follow. If the matter be one in which several people are concerned, the birthday of each must be regarded, and a day that will harmonize with them all must be fixed upon. For a funeral, the birthdays of every living member of the family must be considered, else the funeral will prove fatal to the one with whose birthday this day was not in accord. If one member of the family were born in that year of the cycle which is named the Hare, and the funeral of another member of the family should take place on a day in the cycle named the Dog, then the funeral might prove fatal to him who was born in the year of the Hare, because dogs destroy hares.

Sometimes the horoscope of a child is said to disagree with that of some older or more esteemed member of the family, and then the child is sold or given away to some one who has an accordant horoscope. My attention was once called by a woman whom I had known as childless, to her five-year-old son. Her husband had just bought the boy for her for fourteen pounds, the child's horoscope having been pronounced discordant with that of his own mother, who had been ill ever since his birth. The hitherto childless woman was very happy in her new possession, and the boy was hopping jubilantly around her in a pair of new trousers, while his own mother was grieving to death at the loss of her only son.

Those who leave this world are thought to require material outfit for a journey. The Chinese dress consists chiefly of a pair of loose trousers and a tunic. In summer these constitute the costume of a working-man, even when going to market or to church. Wealthy and literary people wear two or more suits, according to the weather and their occupation. Plain white garments are often worn next the person, and coloured ones over these. The garments of men and of women are much alike, except that women wear a kirtle when in full dress. Paper imitations of all sorts of garments are made, and burned at funerals. Every large town and village has

The Inconvenience of Heathenism. 55

shops whose stock consists solely of such goods. Large quantities are kept on hand ready-made; and paper piece-goods are also kept, and made up to order. The poorest people burn at least four shillings' worth of such goods when a member of the family dies, and the rich often burn more than twenty pounds' worth. The poor burn the paper equipage on the seventh day after the decease, at which time the spirit is supposed to become aware that it is separated from the body, and takes its departure for the land of shades. The rich have a soothsayer, choose a lucky day (some day within a hundred after the decease), and notify their friends and relatives when the burning of apparel will take place. All who come bring offerings to add to the fire. Great quantities of imitation clothing are burned, and also paper boats, horses, sedan-chairs, trunks, mock money, bedding, opium-pipes, rugs, spectacles, images of servants and attendants, and all that a traveller could use in taking a journey to a far country.

These things are supposed to be transmuted, in burning, into the articles which they represent, and to enhance the comfort and wealth of the spirit to whom they are offered. It is thought that the departed will be treated more courteously and leniently by the constables and judges in Hades if he appear there as a rich man with many possessions. Packages of such articles are brought as presents to other spirits, and are burned with those belonging to the newly departed. They are sent to one already in the other world, by one who is going there, just as a person living in China might send a parcel to a friend in England by a mutual acquaintance who was on his way to that country. Such presents are not sent, however, more than three years after the friend's death, as it is said that after three years the spirit no longer wears the clothing supplied by its kindred on earth.

If you ask any of those who sell or burn this paper equipage, how they know that the spirit gets the things that are offered, or why they think that the spirit does not leave the body until the seventh day after death, or why it does not use the paper clothing for a longer period than three years, they will tell you that they do not know. This doctrine is not one that is set forth by their sages nor is it found in books, but it is what their neighbours say and practise, and they follow the custom.

No one will buy these goods nor keep them in his house, except when preparing for a funeral, because of a superstition that to do so would cause a death in the family.

One day I was in one of the shops where these goods are made and sold. The shelves and counters were piled with wonderful imitations of crape, satin, velvet, and brocade, and the shopmen were busy in making these into garments with paste. Soon after, I passed a place where a great heap of such things had just been burned and the wind was scattering the ashes abroad. Then I thought of the poor, naked spirit, that, all unclothed and unhelped by the futile efforts of those who had been its human kin, had drifted, solitary and terrified, out into the great darkness. How unlike its going forth, to that of one who goes knowing that God is, and that in all His universe there is no place where His children need be afraid or lonely!

CHAPTER IX.

SPIRITUALISM.

MANY men and women in China fall at times into a trance followed by frenzy, and are consulted as spirit-mediums or interpreters of the gods, whose mouthpiece they are supposed to become. The trance state is said to be first induced by gazing steadfastly at a piece of gilded paper held near the eyes while one sits at a table on which is a censer containing burning incense. Afterward the familiar spirit may take possession of the medium at any moment and without invitation. The spirit-mediums previously announce, by incoherent talk while in the trance state, what they will do at a certain date, and eager devotees prepare the appliances for the exhibition of what is considered to be supernatural power. Some of their frequent exercises are walking over a bed of live coals, washing in boiling oil, and climbing ladders of knives. The beds of live coals are several tens of feet long, but the coals are not compact, and an agile person can skip speedily over them, treading only in the interspaces. The washing in boiling oil appears marvellous, but is really not a dangerous performance. A large iron pan over a blazing fire contains boiling oil. ·A small towel dipped in cold water in which twelve kinds of flowers have been steeped, lies in a tub beside the pan. The medium rushes along, snatches the towel, plunges it into the oil, instantly draws it out, and rubs herself therewith. The cold water meeting the hot oil makes a mighty commotion, but the towel is scarcely more than warmed, and no danger is incurred in the washing. The ladders of knives may be safely ascended by any one, the knives are blunt edged, and the wooden wedges by which they are fastened into the uprights project above the edges of the knives, and form a safe resting-place for the feet of the climber. Nothing but the horror of the bystanders at so sacrilegious an act has prevented at least one person who was not a spirit-medium from going up these ladders, to prove that the ascent might be made without supernatural aid. The danger lies only in the insecurity of the fastenings holding the ladder in place. I have heard of several mediums who were killed by its fall when at the top. If the medium cuts his feet on the knives, or burns them on the coals, or scalds himself with the oil, the reason given is that some one who has lately borne a son, or married a wife, has looked at him during the performance.

I have among my personal acquaintances several women who have been or are spirit-mediums. One of these resides at Cannon Stand, on the Kit-ie river. The account which she gave of herself was, that for twenty years she had been a spirit-medium, but now she believed that Jesus could and would save her from the powers of darkness. When she was first attacked by the spirits, she had convulsions, and was as one delirious, and while in this state she announced that she would the next morning walk over a bed of burning coals. When she came to herself she trembled and wept, because she thought she should be burnt to death; but, as the people were accustomed to such manifestations,

Spiritualism. 59

they prepared the bed of coals, thirty-five feet long, and at the appointed time she again became frenzied, and walked over it unharmed. Since then, every year when there was to be a pestilence or when cholera was to prevail, she went into this frenzy and cut her tongue with a knife, letting some drops of the blood fall into a hogshead of water. This water the people drank as a specific against contagion. With the rest of the blood she wrote charms which the people pasted upon their door-posts or wore upon their persons, as preventives of evil. Sometimes she predicted that two little girls of the same height would walk the burning road with her, and when she was ready to start, a pair of the girls of the village were impelled to come out of the crowd of spectators, and in spite of themselves to follow her over the fiery path. She also took off her head-cloth dipped it into a pot of boiling oil, and washed herself with it unscathed; but if she scattered any of it on other people it blistered them. While in this condition, she was possessed by the spirit of a female demon, and did its will, not her own. She says that the sensations of being possessed are worse than sea-sickness, which was probably a new and impressive experience to her when she came to my house by boat. She held communication with this spirit at any time, and people came constantly for consultation with it through her. She received no money for her services as interpreter, but told what offerings were to be brought to propitiate the spirit, and she kept the food which remained after the ceremonies of worship were completed.

Soon after she met the Bible-women and heard the gospel from them, a man came to get, from the spirit, advice concerning a sick child; but she took the incense-pot used in her practices, and threw it with all its belongings into the river. Her adherents said she had gone crazy, but she told them she had only just become sane.

Almost every village has one or more spirit-mediums, each having his or her familiar spirit. If spiritualism is good, China ought to be the most enlightened and holy of countries. But, though spirit-mediums are so numerous, no practical wisdom has come from the other world through them. Here, as elsewhere, departed wise men ignore this method of communication with human kind. Confucius has not through them imparted any additional exhortations concerning the duties of the five relations, and Shakspeare has not used them for sending a new poem to his compatriots. Hwang Ti, who invented Chinese boats, has suggested no improvement in junks, and Watt has added nothing to the steam-engine. Yu, who drained the country after a great flood, has given no useful hints for later inundations, but has been as silent as Morse has been concerning a more perfect telegraph insulator. Among Mongols as among Saxons, philanthropists and writers and statesmen have died with unfinished work on hand, and have made no use of the spirit-mediums to tell how it should be completed. Should Mencius send maxims as wise as those he wrote when in the flesh, and Milton a poem as grand as Paradise Lost, and Fuhhi a new musical instrument, and Bacon more perfect laws of investigation, there will be reason for holding in esteem the mediums through which such valuable communications are sent. But while "spiritual mediums" of the most authentic sort swarm in China, they fail, as in other places, to convey any useful knowledge to mankind.

CHAPTER X.

THE KITCHEN-GOD.

THE gods are legion. These are the great images in the large temples and the odd fragments of idols in shrines; the local deities, of which every village, field, and mountain has its own; the invisible controllers of the thunder, the rain, the harvest, and the elements; the spirits of all the dead, and especially of one's ancestors; and besides these every strange object, and the site of every inexplicable phenomenon is worshipped. Oddly shaped stones, queerly gnarled roots, fantastic bits of wood, waifs brought on the tide, are all gods. A fisherman found a mass of half-decayed oyster-shells, the shape of which was thought to resemble a lion, and for generations that was worshipped in his house. On the bank of a stream where some bamboos were cut down, the hollow stumps were filled with water, by capillary action through its fibrous roots. This was considered wonderful, and travellers along the road stopped to burn incense and prostrate themselves before the mysterious deity residing among these bamboos.

All the chief gods have their birthdays on which they are specially worshipped, as well as at the great festivals, and at the new and the full of each moon.

Many of the greater gods have representatives in the family, and ashes from the incense-pots in the temples are frequently brought and worshipped in the houses.

But, whatever else may be absent from a pagan household, Su Meng Kong is not. He is the god of the kitchen, and none would dare to set up housekeeping without him. He has been a god for hundreds of years, and all know the legend concerning him.

A poor man married, and soon became rich, but he discarded the wife that had brought him good luck, and as she wandered along the road, she came to a solitary hut, in which an old man sat. She told this old man her sad story, and he asked her to be his wife. She lived with him in the hut, and he prospered and grew rich, and built a large, fine house. When the kitchen-range was partially made, a man came begging to the door, and she discovered in him her former husband. While she was giving him some money, her present husband approached, and the former husband hid in the kitchen-range and was never seen more. He turned into a god and is one to this day. In some families he has no image set up, and the incense-sticks burned in worshipping him are stuck in the crevices of the range chimney. Many put his image in the main room of the house. His birthday is the fourteenth of the seventh month, and on that day every family worships him, each in its own house. On the twenty-fourth day of the last month of the year, when the gods are supposed to go off for a ten days' holiday, a paper horse and other travelling equipments are burned for his use during his journey to make his annual report to the superior gods. A lamp is kept constantly burning during the first days of the new year, to indicate that the family are waiting to welcome him whenever he returns. Children who have been away from home, on their return, after greeting their parents, worship Su Meng Kong. If the house-mother rears fat

The Kitchen-God.

pigs, she credits her success to his good will, and makes suitable thank-offerings to him when the pigs are sold.

When the father of a family dies, and the ancestral property is divided among the sons, the eldest gets the image of Su Meng Kong, the second gets the censer that stands before him, and the others get portions of the ashes from the censer. Each then supplies what is lacking in his own religious outfit, and sets up his god, and worships it before cooking a meal in his own house.

CHAPTER XI.

THE INFLUENCE OF THE IDOLS.

IT is customary, near the close of the Chinese year, to take the tutelary deity out from his temple, and to carry him through the principal streets of the town. A gilded, open sedan-chair is provided for his conveyance, with bearers dressed in gorgeous and fanciful costumes. A band of musicians heads the procession, and the throng follows with banners of strange device. The end of the route is an open-air theatre, at which the god is the honoured guest and spectator. This outing is supposed to gratify the idol who has for many months been sitting in gloom and cobwebs, and who may be supposed to be weary of the monotony of his existence. His passage is, moreover, thought to have a salutary influence in the streets through which he is carried.

Long ago, in the village of Iam Chau, a sum of money was contributed, and placed in the hands of a village elder to pay the expense of this annual festival; but this master of ceremonies was a gambler, and immediately lost all the money in play. Days passed, and as the theatre and procession were not forthcoming, the contributors became urgent that he should perform his duties, and so constantly harried him that he was at his wits' end for excuses wherewith to pacify them. One of the causes of the urgency of the people was the fear that

The Influence of the Idols.

the god would become ill-tempered and harmful if longer neglected. As the New-year approached the clamour increased, but with neither money nor credit he was unable to furnish the usual equipments for the god's journey. So, early one morning, he went to the temple, took the god on his back, and started off on the established rounds. An amazed crowd soon followed him, and some attempted to take the god from his back. After many struggles and escapes, he was at last driven to the shore, where he was shut in between the crowd and the sea, and then the contest ended in the waves, where the god was jerked to and fro, to the peril of its gilding and the destruction of its limbs. Thence the victors took it to the temple, where it was repaired and reinstated, amid the fears of the alarmed populace over whom its influence was supposed to extend. But the ensuing year proved to be a most auspicious one, with abundant crops, and no epidemics. The public weal was then accredited to the extraordinary treatment and sea-bath that the god had received, and so on every anniversary of that performance its peculiar features have been imitated in that village to the present day.

The Chinese sometimes make an idol the umpire in a dispute. When there is neither testimony nor evidence whereby an ordinary magistrate can decide a case, a suspected person may go before a god, and there invoke a curse upon himself if he be guilty. If no evil follow, he is held to be innocent. Of course it often happens that in the court of these wooden judges the hardihood of the culprit enables him to evade punishment, and the misfortune of the innocent subjects him to condemnation. Sometimes the god appears to inflict chastisement, and afterwards the injustice of the judgment is discovered, whereupon the god becomes very unpopular, until some other accident re-establishes it in the confidence of its worshippers.

Several years ago, a man took passage in a boat running between Swatow and Kit-ie, cities forty-two miles apart. It was in the time when clan feuds and piracy made travelling very unsafe; and the passenger handed a packet containing his money of the value of ten pounds to the owner and captain of the boat for secure keeping. The captain, as was his custom with valuables committed to his care by passengers, put the money away in his own cabin, which was in the stern of the boat, and had no entrance except a trap-door, on which the captain stood when steering his vessel. When the boat reached its destination, the passenger came to get his money, but it could not be found. The captain being responsible for the loss, it behoved him to discover the thief. As he had not been away from the door of his cabin during the whole journey, and as no one but the man at the bow had the right to enter or had been seen to go into his cabin, he at once accused him of the theft. The bowman declared himself innocent, and, in the altercation that ensued, offered to go before a certain renowned idol and invoke a curse upon himself if he were guilty. The captain acceded to this proposal, and agreed to acquit the bowman if the god did so. So they went, with many interested spectators and with offerings, to the temple, and the bowman swore that he was guiltless, invoking the god with imprecations, and calling upon it to make him break his leg as he passed out from the temple, if he had lied. Surely it so happened. As he passed out from the temple, he stumbled over the stone door-sill and broke his leg. His guilt was believed to be proven; and great fear of the idol fell upon the bystanders and on those to whom they made their report.

But on returning to his boat, the captain, rummaging in his cabin, found the parcel of money in an obscure crevice, where he had put it when he left Swatow. He returned to his bowman, acknowledged the wrong done him, paid for a doctor and medicines till the leg was healed, and trusted the idol no more.

A poor man, near Chiang Lim, had a son studying under the direction of a priest in a Buddhist temple. One day the man went to carry a bag of rice to the little student, and shortly after his departure from the temple, the priest missed a fowl which he was rearing and training to fight. He accused the man, who declared that he was guiltless of the theft and invoked the curse of the god upon himself if he spoke falsely. He stood before the god and said, "If I took the fowl, may I break an arm as I go out of thy presence." As he left the temple he stumbled on the steps and fell, breaking his arm. Shortly afterwards, the priest was moving some rice-baskets that were piled on the temple floor, and on lifting an inverted one, out jumped the fowl. He then remembered having covered it in that way the day before.

CHAPTER XII.

THE STONE PRINCESS AND HER TRAIN.

SOME hundreds of years ago there lived, in the Fokien Province, a maiden whose father, brothers, and betrothed husband were all traders. Once when she was at home with her mother, and the men of her household were away at sea, she dreamed that she saw their three junks tossed in the storm and about to be wrecked. Swimming out to succour them, she seized two of the junks with her hands, and one between her teeth. She was making her way safely homeward with them, when she heard her mother call her. In order to answer, she had to open her mouth, and thus she lost one junk from her hold, and brought only two into port.

Many days after the dream, the mariners returned, and reported that they had encountered a fearful tempest, in which one of their junks was lost, while two marvellously outrode the storm.

This, with a long and honourable widowhood, was the cause of the apotheosis of this woman, who is now worshipped under the title of " The Queen of Heaven." Her temples are numerous and rich. The oldest temple in the city of Swatow, belonging to this goddess, was repaired in 1879, at an expense of two hundred pounds ; and a grand procession escorted her regilded and bedizened image through the main streets of the town, to reinstate it in its niche. The eight chief streets vied each with the others in the magnificence of the escort provided. All business ceased, the wares that usually cumber the sides of the streets were removed, and banners and transparencies made a gorgeous awning overhead. Six thousand pounds were expended on the equipments for the procession, as much as two hundred pounds being contributed by a single individual. Thousands of persons came from the country around, and thronged all the standing-room to gaze at the procession as it passed. The goddess herself, borne in a splendid sedan, and accompanied by her two hideous servants, one with enormous ears that are supposed to hear a thousand miles, and the other with glaring eyes that are supposed to see a similar distance, did not excite manifest enthusiasm, nor receive special attention from the crowd.

ORDER OF ONE-EIGHTH OF THE PROCESSION.

Two trumpets making wild-beast cries.
One horizontal four-character scroll carried by two bearers.
Two large lanterns carried by two men.
Eight title or degree boards, two abreast.
Twenty halberds, silver and gold gilt, two abreast.
Eighteen horizontal four-character scrolls, two abreast, carried by well-clad men, all wearing spectacles.
Two vertical scrolls.
Eight men in fine drab silk clothes and straw hats, two abreast.
A band of twelve musicians, under an awning.
Nine Swatow merchants in mandarin dress.
Band.
Old bronze vase on table, four bearers.
Two horizontal scrolls.
Nine large banners, highly embroidered, and borne by men with enormous queues laid in coils on their heads.

Coolie carrying tea and refreshments.
Gongs, cymbals, and string band.
Six horizontal scrolls, two abreast.
A paper horse and girl mounted on a wagon.
Ten small silk embroidered umbrellas.
Band.
Platform with carved bamboo-root birds.
Two guards.
Platform with tree-roots cut to resemble five geese.
Music.
Platform with tree-roots cut to resemble dog and pups.
Two guards.
Paper lion on a wagon.
Young warrior on horseback.
Paper lion, cub, and globe on wheels.
Music.
Young warrior on horseback.
Two boy warriors.
Paper dolphin in chariot drawn by two apes.
Music.
Boy warrior on horseback.
Two boy warriors on foot.
Horizontal four-character screen.
Music.
Platform with black jade ornaments.
Two guards.
Platform with white jade ornaments, four bearers.
Music.
Platform with red and white coral ornaments.
Gongs.
Very fine chariot with two young girls, one sitting down, and the other supported on a peacock's head; a fine example of balancing.
Music.
Platform with a boy standing and holding out a fan at arm's length, on which a girl stands without any visible support.
Music, guards, and marshals.
Two magnificent large umbrellas.
Chariot with boy and girl; boy supporting the girl on a sword which he holds at arm's length; no visible support.

The Stone Princess and her Train. 71

Music.
Boy balancing a coloured umbrella on his elbow, and girl standing on rim of umbrella ; no visible support or counterbalance.
Two umbrellas highly embroidered.
Music.
A paper giant nine feet high, very good imitation.
Eight tablets borne by little boys, two abreast ; the boys very nicely dressed ; tablet trays highly embroidered.
Four boy warriors, well armed.
Two vertical triangular bannerets.
Platform with a very fine miniature temple, in blue enamel and gold, twelve bearers.
Five large embroidered umbrellas.
Two small temples with tablets in the interior.
Music.
Four boys carrying tablets on trays.
Nine merchants dressed as mandarins.
Two horizontal scrolls.
Eight boy warriors on horseback in Indian file, each supported by two young warriors on foot.
Young girl on horseback.
Refreshments.
Platform with two girls working at a bean-curd mill.
Two horizontal banners.
Platform with set piece of coral and rocks, on which are mounted two pretty girls.
Boy mandarin on horseback.
String band.
Grand temple in black and gold, eighteen bearers.
Four vertical, triangular, highly embroidered banners.
Set piece, "All amongst the flowers," a young girl and a live monkey.
Four boys carrying handsome tapestry screens.
Eighteen gentry in dark-blue dresses.
Grand dragon, upwards of ninety feet long, borne by twenty-two men.
Gongs, drums, and cymbals.
Boys on horseback as warriors and emperors.
Two horizontal four-character scrolls.
Refreshments, tea, tobacco, and betel.
Magnificent umbrella with figures in relief.

CHAPTER XIII.

BUDDHIST NUNS.

AMONG the villages, one not infrequently sees a woman in a grey cotton tunic and conical splint hat, with a shaven head and natural feet, and carrying a bag and basket on her arm. Her attire distinguishes her from other Chinese women. The long grey gown and shaven head are the badges of her religious order, that of a Buddhist nun. The bag holds the rice, and the basket the fruit and vegetables, given her at the doors of the houses before which she halts. She is supposed to have more intimate friendship with Buddha than those have who dwell outside his temple, and all who give to the servant will get favours from the lord of the house. Devotion in the believer is not a criterion of the truth of a creed. The Buddhist nun's bag is always well filled, although little good comes to the donors of its contents.

In the gleanings of her morning walk, the nun has enough for herself and for other nuns too young or too old to go out and gather for themselves. Her home is a temple, sometimes extensive in its grounds, fine in its architecture, and elegant in its appurtenances. It is built by one rich family, or by the contributions of many persons, in the hope of making merit which shall be put to their credit in the next world. It has a main building, in which are immense figures of Buddha, and lesser halls with images of their saints. Before these the nuns chant

Buddhist Nuns. 73

liturgies three times a day. Their sacred writings are in Chinese letters, translated from the Buddhist books brought to China from India in the year 63 A.D. Around the chief temple are courts with small apartments, where the nuns sleep and work. These women are the only inmates of the place. They sew and spin, and bring up children to be nuns like themselves. These child-nuns are not such by the will of God, nor by their own will; but they are orphans by the will of some man, and nuns by the will of some woman. They are sold to the nunnery, when two or three years old, for less than a pound apiece; and the nuns, each buying as many as she can support, bring them up. Sometimes a nun thus has as many as twenty little girls under her immediate care, and subject to no authority but hers. The nuns, being well-to-do in the world, do not take such children as would be thrown or given away, but buy those that are past the first diseases of infancy, and healthy and attractive. As soon as the girls are old enough, they are taught to weave, and embroider, and read. A good teacher is employed to instruct them, and they often become good scholars.

At fifteen, the little girl ceases to eat animal food, has her head clean-shaven, and puts on the dress of a nun. It is said that no coercion is used in keeping girls in the nunnery, but that none of them ever choose to leave it and return to their parents. They are much more comfortable in the nunnery than they could be with the poverty-stricken parents who sold them.

The nuns frequently make long excursions in their own boats, bringing home boat-loads of fruit or vegetables. They weave with skill, and embroider exquisitely, and are almost the only women who know how to read.

They are called to chant at death-beds, to dispel the evil influences in streets and houses, and they receive pay for special petitions to their gods. Their incomes are large and their lives easy. In general, they appear strong, portly, and comfortable beyond other Chinese women.

The nunneries are regarded with reverence by the ignorant and superstitious, but it is whispered among the wise that they are not the religious and respectable haunts they nominally represent. We hear not infrequently of a nunnery having been broken up by the civil authorities, on account of its vice.

In a country where no census is taken, and no statistics compiled, it is difficult to ascertain the number of nuns in the population. But one may see a dozen nunneries within a day's journey; and in one forenoon I visited three nunneries, having a hundred nuns in them. The abbess in one of them was seventy-five years old, and had been in the nunnery seventy-two years. All the women with whom I privately spoke had been in the nunnery from infancy. The friendly old abbess gave me every opportunity to speak of what she called "God's doctrines," but when I suggested that a native female teacher might come and stay there a few days, she responded that it would be wholly contrary to the customs of the place should she allow any meat-eater to lodge there. She said she herself was old and had laid by enough to live on, and so she could believe my words; but the other nuns could not believe, because, if they did, they would have nothing to eat. She would herself come to my home and be taught, and I could come and tell my doctrine to the nuns, and they could judge for themselves whether it were something for which it was worth while to starve.

CHAPTER XIV.

LOAN ASSOCIATIONS.

A COMMON method of raising money to meet a pecuniary emergency is to form a loan society. This society is temporary and voluntary, and its benefits are equal to all its members. The capital invested in it varies from five shillings to fifty pounds, and the number of members from three to twenty. The leader in the formation of the company is its president, who must make good all losses to its members. He is therefore careful in admitting persons, and must himself possess sufficient to meet the responsibilities. Both men and women form such associations, each sex by itself unless the association be limited to a single family circle. The occasion of its formation may be the buying of a field, or a coffin, or a wife, the setting up of a shop, the paying of a debt, or the expense of a lawsuit. The one who wants to use a certain sum of money goes among his friends and finds who will join the loan society. He gives information to each, concerning the names of others who will join, the amount of each share and the time of payment. He then makes a supper to which all the members of the society are invited, and each guest lends the host one share. In a month, a half-year, or at whatever time has been agreed upon, every member, except the president, bids on the next loan, and he who bids highest gets it.

The bids are sealed and are opened by the president in the presence of all the members. The highest bidder at once pays the amount bid to each member, except him who has already had the loan, and every member then pays to this highest bidder a sum equal to what each paid before to the president. So the loan continues to circulate, each who has not yet received it being allowed to bid, and no one who has once had it being allowed to bid a second time. Those who have once had the loan receive no interest and the one who receives it last pays no interest, in the form of a bid, to the others.

Say A, B, C, and D form such a mutual loan society. A gives a supper, costing perhaps a shilling to the other three, and they each pay A four shillings. In a month, B, C, and D bid for the next loan, and B, bidding higher than C or D, pays them each the amount he has bid, sixpence, and A, C, and D each pay B four shillings. The following month, C bids highest and secures the loan; and in the fourth month, A, B, and C, each pay four shillings to D. Each of the members has now received as much as he has paid out, less interest or the amount of his bid, and the association is dissolved.

I know a farmer, somewhat advanced in years, who thus raised the money with which he paid for his wife. Having heard, through a female relative, of a widow with a young son, who could be secured by him for five pounds, he formed a loan society of ten members, the shares being ten shillings, and with the sum thus obtained, he paid for his wife. Afterwards he paid ten shillings every three months, to some member of the society till all were paid.

A woman who wishes to buy a new tunic, and lacks the necessary cash, may get it in the same way.

CHAPTER XV.

OUR APOTHECARY.

WE have among our church-members a thriving druggist, whose shop is in the city of Swatow. Having ascertained that he had time and inclination to show us his stock of medicines, I went with a friend to see them. The shop, after the manner of Chinese shops, is enclosed on three sides only, and has the whole front open to the street. The counter runs the whole length of the front of the shop, except in a narrow place left for egress, and the purchaser is expected to stand in the street, and ask over the counter for what he wants. The cases for drugs, which cover the inner wall, can be touched with one hand, while the counter is reached with the other. The stock on hand is valued at about two hundred pounds, and many a shop with goods of greater value would be no less narrow. Behind and above the shop, the druggist's family (consisting of his wife, three children, and two clerks) live, and exercise hospitality toward travelling church-members, in a space scarcely wider than a hay-wagon.

Many villagers come to Swatow on business; and, though foreigners have been visible in its streets for twenty years, there are always those who think one a curiosity worth observing, so we had been in the shop but a few minutes when the whole front was lined with silent and interested gazers at the two foreign ladies who had come to look at the native drugs. Moreover, the wife was making tea, and filling the place with the smoke from her open and pipeless furnace. These discomforts, added to the heat of a summer afternoon on the Tropic of Cancer, caused us to relinquish our design of making an accurate list in Chinese and English of all the drugs, and to take note of only those which were specially curious.

Among a great variety of barks, tubers, bulbs, roots, leaves, and seeds, we found, in separate compartments, the stamens, petals, and seed-vessels of the lotus water-lily; unhusked rice and wheat, sprouted and then dried; the flowers of the honeysuckle; the leaves of the arbor-vitæ; various species of sea-weed; bones of the cuttle-fish; the cast skins of locusts; the pith of a large reed; dried caterpillars, snails, and worms; fungi from decayed wood; chrysalides of moths and butterflies; scales of the armadillo; shavings of the horns of goat, ibex, and deer; skin of the rhinoceros and the elephant; tigers' bones, charred; silk-worms; the shell of the box-turtle; the gall-bladder of a bear, valued at two pounds, and used as a tonic; the horn of a rhinoceros, valued at twelve shillings a piece of three inches in length; centipedes, six inches long, stretched and dried on splints; medicated tea in small, hard cakes, used in infusion as a sudorific.

Our obliging host said there were many other drugs in the shop, among them seed-pearls, and snake-skins, and minerals; but we had not time to see them all, and having bought a box of medicated tea, and five tiny bottles of crystallized peppermint-oil, we took our departure.

Our Apothecary.

The Chinese have little knowledge of anatomy, physiology, or hygiene, and do not practise surgery; but four thousand years of experience have given them some just ideas concerning the uses of herbs, and they often apply these with great skill in poultices and in teas. No such thing is known as a medical education, but every literary man is more or less a physician. Specialists are common. Some families have a knowledge how to cure a particular disease, and this knowledge is kept a secret, and is handed down as an heirloom from generation to generation.

One of my native acquaintances is wholly deaf in one ear, and the cause of her deafness is a fair specimen of Chinese medical diagnosis and practice. Years ago this woman caught a severe cold, followed by much headache. She went to a Chinese doctor for advice, and was told that her headache was caused by a disease, in the form of a small kernel in her head, and that the only way to cure her would be to let the disease out through a hole made either in her eye or her ear. She thought it better to lose the latter; and so, instead of having her eyeball punctured, she had her ear deeply probed, breaking the tympanum. She has been deaf ever since, but the headaches were not cured.

CHAPTER XVI.

RAMBLINGS.

IN Southern China, all travelling is done in boats, in sedan-chairs, or on foot, and the rate of speed seldom averages above three miles an hour, by any mode of conveyance. Food and bedding must be included in the luggage, and the itinerary must be carefully planned, else one may be without shelter at nightfall. Of boats, there is a special style for nearly every stream, varying from the simplest raft to the elaborately constructed and ornate junk. One of medium size and considerable comfort is that called the "Hakka boat," which has usually a crew of five men. It is of fir, about fifty feet long and eight feet wide, with a hold three feet deep, over which a flooring of loose boards is laid. In the middle of the boat are two apartments, high enough to stand in, roofed semicircularly with splint basket-work, and thatched with leaves of the edible bamboo. The three partitions, forming the walls of the two apartments, are often grotesquely carved and gorgeously painted. The tiller is a wide paddle, projecting ten feet behind the boat, after passing through a hole in an upright post, which turns on a pivot in the stern. The prow rises, by an inclined plane, six feet above the deck, and up this the boatmen walk barefooted, then turn around, and come back almost head downward, each bearing his weight on a long pole, one end of which is fixed against his shoulder, while the other is inserted in the sandy bottom of the shallow stream. Thus the boat is pushed forward just half as fast and half as far as the boatmen walk. In deeper water, the boat is drawn along by ropes tied to its mast, the boatmen walking in a tow-path on shore; or it is rowed, the boatman standing at the oar as does a Venetian gondolier. When there is a favourable wind, they set a bamboo mat perpendicularly on the top of the boat, and stretch cloth sails above and beside it. Many boats, sailing together, make a striking scene; for, though they be torn and dirty, they are always, like Italian beggars, picturesque in their rags. The boatmen have a peculiar and not unmusical cry, which the steersman shouts and the bowman echoes. This is their manner of whistling for the wind. Even with all these diverse modes of propulsion, progress is slow; but if one gets a boat that is new, and free from vermin; if the smoke from the cooking, which must be done for all on board, is well shut off; if there are no opium-smokers among the crew; if no unsavoury cargo has been stowed in the hold, as a private business venture by the boatmen; and if the boat has been carefully furnished with everything that is necessary during the trip, one may travel very comfortably.

Those who travel by boat sleep in their floating domicile; but those who travel in a sedan-chair must seek lodgings in an inn, where nothing is furnished except a bedstead and a fire by which to cook. The chair is usually carried by two coolies; but if the occupant be portly, he will soon be set down, with the remark that a person so highly favoured by the gods should have three bearers. The chair-coolies are of the lowest class in

China, and are so obstreperous and foul-mouthed that one who deals with them in travelling soon comes to believe that the canon debarring their descendants to the third generation from the literary examinations is a reasonable one, founded on the law of heredity.

The cost of boat and men is about four shillings a day, while the cost of travel by sedan-chair is about threepence per mile. A chair is not always to be obtained. A boat can usually be secured by a man, though a woman may sometimes fail to get a passage. Returning homeward from a station upon the Swatow Bay, I one night found a head wind and surging waves opposing me. After beating against these until dark, my boatmen declared it impossible to make any progress, and said that we must run in beside the shore, and wait until the wind should veer and the tide turn. I had to decide whether I would toss all night where I was, or call a smaller boat, with strong oarsmen, to take me the remaining three miles. I decided to have a fishing-boat called as soon as one was sighted; and, after some waiting, a little tub came along, manned by three stalwart rowers. A prolonged bargaining was terminated by their agreeing to take one passenger to my landing-place for thirteenpence halfpenny. They came alongside, and I stepped out from my cabin, when suddenly the little tub paddled off with might and main; the rowers exclaiming simultaneously to each other, "It is a foreign *lady!* It is a teach*eress!* It is a *woman!*" No bribe would induce them to return. Their grave response to all ridicule of their sudden fright and flight was, that if they were to carry even so much of womankind as a female infant a span long, their boat would catch no fish for many days thereafter. Happily, we were near shore; and with my long-known and trusty steersman as "guide, philosopher, and friend," I sped on foot over the hills to my home.

In China, one who cannot walk is subject to perpetual extortion. There, as in other countries, independence secures service on reasonable terms. The roads being always narrow and rough, walking is often the pleasantest and sometimes the only way of reaching one's destination. Pedestrian tours are interesting, taking one along the foot of ranges of hills whose slopes are flecked with plantations of dark green firs and pale green pine-apples. The fir-trees are burned into charcoal, and the gleam of the pits may be seen from afar on dark nights. The pine-apple leaves yield a fibre which is woven into coarse cloth, used for summer garments. Paths only a foot wide divide the patches of rice and sugar-cane, and border the plots of hemp, pulse, indigo, millet, and wheat. The arable land is worth from eighty to a hundred and twenty pounds an acre, and is cultivated with extreme economy. Shallow streams must be waded, or the traveller may be carried across pick-a-back by a good-natured and strong companion. Neither natives nor foreigners can safely rely on friendly offices of any sort among strangers, but from acquaintances the utmost courtesy may be expected. The poorest offer hot boiled sweet potatoes, begging the wayfarer to stay his stomach with their scanty fair, while those of larger means prepare a feast and urge a prolonged stay. In every case, the hostess immediately proceeds to make tea, and no protestations can persuade her to forego this customary sign of welcome. She is apt to light the fire in a chimneyless earthen stove in a corner of the room, filling the whole apartment with smoke. When the tea is made, it is offered with confectionery, peanut-candy, or parched rice cohering in a mixture of sugar and lard. If the guest was expected, she is sure to offer also hot soup, consisting of sweet syrup, in which pellets of dough or whole eggs are floating. When the traveller goes on his way, some members of the household accompany him on the road. He begs them not to go a mile, and they go with him twain, and can hardly be induced to turn back.

On the way from Toa Pho, I saw a woman going along the street wailing aloud. She was hobbling slowly on her bound feet, supported by a long staff, and was telling her wrongs in a piercing wail. A native preacher who was with me, although unacquainted with the person or the place, at once informed me that the woman was a widow, who had had her husband's property taken from her by his brothers. She was, after the manner of women thus wronged, appealing to the public for redress. That portion of the public seen by me paid no attention to her, but went silently on with its previous occupations. It is not the habit of Chinese people to put forth any chivalrous effort in behalf of the unfortunate.

Passing through a street in Kui Su, we were followed by a beggar whose clothes scarcely covered his begrimed body. But he did not rely solely on his wretched looks in getting money from people. He stretched one hand for alms, and extended the other filled with writhing snakes. Timid people soon paid him for going away. It seems that sympathy is not a fund whereon beggars may largely draw, and so they make themselves so horrible that shopkeepers and householders will quickly give something to be rid of them. One is frequently seen with his tongue protruded as far as possible, and a knife apparently stuck vertically through it. Besmeared with blood from head to foot, he is sufficiently disgusting

Ramblings.

to make even those who know the knife to be a sham, willing to hasten him out of sight at any cost. Sometimes beggars bring heavy stones with them, and lying down upon the doorstep, drop these stones from the arm's-length upon their own chests, wailing until the master of the house gives them the cash they seek.

In going by chair to Kau Lam, the road was so narrow that the leaves of the sugar-cane, growing in the fields on either hand, often swept both sides of the chair at once; and if we met another traveller, he or we must leave the road in order to pass. In going fifteen miles we went through thirty-five villages, and this is one of the most sparsely populated portions of the country. In going up the river, we counted sixty-seven villages within view while our boat was moving three miles; and from a hill two hundred feet above the plain, we counted eighty-five villages dotting the rice-fields. Some of these villages have a population of ten thousand or more, and cities of from thirty to three hundred thousand are not far distant.

At Hue Sua I asked old Sui, the first woman in that region to accept Christianity, how many Christian women there were in the community. She said there were twenty, and gave the name, age, and place of residence of each. Four of the number were in heaven. I went over the list, and said, "Then there are sixteen women who are members of the church here." "Aye," said Sui, "there are twenty." I remarked, that I had seen twelve of the sixteen, and Sui responded, "Aye, teacheress, you have seen twelve of the twenty." Like Wordsworth's little maid, she had her way, and always counted the sisters who were in heaven.

On arriving at Kau Lam, we found the family of the

old preacher Tue expecting us, and they had cleaned the house for our benefit. The rubbish had all been removed from the middle of the floor to the corners, and the village school, kept by a Christian, had been dismissed two days earlier than its usual vacation, that we might sleep in the school-house and receive our many visitors there. During all our stay, our domicile was filled with eager observers of the strange foreign guests, and many of these became attentive pupils. Tue's family made manifest the great difference between monotheists and pagans. Living in a hamlet, where all the dwellings are merely huts built of sun-dried blocks of mud, with the same dress, the same blood, the same cares as their neighbours, they are so superior to their kin as to seem to be of a different race. The kindness which marks the intercourse of the members of the family, their courtesy, their morality, their intelligence, the considerate way in which its men treat its women, all show the effect of Christianity acting upon them through more than one generation. If those who in Christian lands despise and malign Christ, should suddenly have taken from them all the good that has come to them through Him, with what bitter repentance would they bewail their loss! Those who have not lived in countries where His light has never shined cannot fully realize how much of the brightness and sweetness of their lives is the result of His influence in the world.

The ancestor of the two thousand persons living in Kau Lam came to that place from some other region, about two hundred years ago. He married and had two sons, whose descendants all these people are. As Chinese law forbids the marriage of those having the same surname, the men of this clan go to other villages to get their wives, and marry their daughters to men of other tribes. It is said that almost as many men of this clan have gone abroad as have stayed at home. At a small estimate, the single ancestor of this clan has now three thousand living descendants.

On the way to Po Chan, we visited the grave of a church-member who had lately died. His name was Faithful, and there was much about him beside his name to remind one of his prototype in "Pilgrim's Progress." He lived in a great and wicked city, surrounded by persecuting heathen, his business was constantly hindered, and his life sometimes endangered by his unwavering adherence to a religion unlike that of his neighbours. He never swerved in his allegiance to his Lord, and he has gained the reward that is prepared for those who endure to the end. Many of the Christians, when about to die, give orders that the words "A disciple of Jesus" shall be graven on their tombstones. Such was the last request of Faithful; but his son disregarded his wish, and there is nought but pagan symbols on the stone. That does not matter. When the Lord comes to gather His elect from the four corners of the earth, He will know without considering epitaphs where to look for His own.

A few years ago, Faithful, who was a sugar-merchant, went to Shanghai on business. When he returned he came to see me, and I asked him if, while he was in Shanghai, he went to any of the chapels there, or met any of the native Christians. He replied that one day when he had leisure, he went and found a chapel, and there was an old man in it who appeared to be a preacher, and that he sat and talked with him for two hours, and enjoyed it very much. "But," said I, "you do not speak the Shanghai dialect, and the old man in the chapel did not speak the Swatow dialect, so you and he could not understand each other in talking." "Oh," responded Faithful, "it is true that I could not speak his language, nor he mine; but when he said *Jesus*, I knew what he was talking about, and when I said *Jesus*, I could tell by the way he nodded his head that he understood me, and so we talked for two hours together, and I did enjoy it very much."

Mr. Ong, who walked to Po Chan with me, pointed out with great cheerfulness on the way a hillock where he intended immediately to build a tomb for himself and wife. The provident Chinese prepare such things long before they expect to use them. On my returning home from a two weeks' trip, my cook smilingly informed me that he had taken advantage of the leisure afforded by my absence, and had had two excellent coffins made, and had presented them to his grandparents, who had received these testimonials with much satisfaction, and had bestowed on him much praise for his filial piety.

Going one morning to a village that lies among steep barren hills, whose slopes are covered with boulders that seem to be moving downward in a slow, mighty torrent, I saw on the outskirts an old woman gathering herbs. She said she was going to make a wash for her daughter-in-law's sore eyes, and she asked me if I had any medicine that would cure blindness. I told her I would go to her house and there tell her what sort of medicine I had, and she led me to her home, a new and almost clean white hut among many brown and ill-smelling ones. Her neighbours saw us going in, and many of them, with small dirty children in their arms, crowded in to inquire what remedy I could offer for their varied ills. They were deeply interested in hearing about a revealed and not distant country in which there is no more pain. That country seemed very attractive to me also, as a boy just as high as my shoulder kept rubbing his frowzy head thereon, while a smaller child tried to thrust his grimy little pate under my arm, and an old woman, a leper from head to foot, stood before me persistently endeavouring to clasp my hands, and asserting that I had grown old fast since she last saw me.

Passing on to another village, I told a woman who sat at her door making sweet-potato flour, that I had a pleasant and important message for her, which I would communicate if she would exclude all the men and children, and admit all the women who should come to the door. She at once assented, and I stationed two boatmen at the entrance to assist in carrying out the arrangement. This is the only plan by which I can secure quiet congregations. The children swarm like locusts, and unless they are firmly excluded they take up the room which may be filled by more appreciative hearers, and by their noise and squabbling make teaching difficult. When the women see that national notions of propriety are adhered to, and that no men are admitted to our presence, they come pouring in from the doorways around, and we have those hearers who most need us, and whom we can most effectively teach. So it was in this house. Ten women sat down to listen, and others stood peering in at the door, too timid or too much prejudiced against new notions for a nearer approach. One old woman listened with peculiar earnestness, and several times asked me to repeat a sentence that she might remember it after I was gone. When our session was finally broken up by the men-folk coming in with farm produce, this old woman hobbled slowly off homeward, and as she went I heard her saying, as if to fix the name firmly in her memory, "Jesus, the Lord; Jesus, the Lord; Jesus, the Lord." She had never heard this name before, and perhaps she will never hear it again; but it may be that when she is about to cross over into the next world, she will there on the border of that vast, unknown region, recall this name, and cry out for "Jesus, the Lord," and that He, who when on earth never failed to respond to such a call, will come and take her into His kingdom.

CHAPTER XVII.

NATIVE FEMALE EVANGELISTS.

IT would seem that woman ought to be foremost in obedience to all Christ's commands, including the Great Commission, because for woman He does more than for man. The next world's glory is promised alike to both sexes; but in this world the benefits of His Salvation are experienced more fully by woman, who, where brute force dominates, is always in unjust subjection. I think that women owe what is most precious in their lives to Jesus of Nazareth. The fact that there are some women in the world to-day who need dread no wrong, who may partake of any intellectual good the world offers, who are sure of the utter loyalty of those who are theirs, is due to the fact that eighteen hundred years ago the Son of God came down among men. Of all ingrates there is none so traitorous as is she who fails to acknowledge her indebtedness to the Christ who has given her, what no pagan woman possesses, security in her rights as a human being without regard to her personal power to maintain them. A true Christianity can never debar woman from showing her gratitude to her Saviour by setting Him forth as the true and sufficient Helper of her sex, both for the life that now is and the life that is to come. A true missionary spirit strives to give the gospel to the neediest, and women are the neediest in heathen lands.

Since we do this work in obedience to the command, "Go, preach the gospel to every creature," we may justly infer that the method which brings the gospel to the greatest number of creatures, is that which our Lord would think the best. There are many methods which are good; but the question is not what is good, but what is best; not how we can do something for the salvation of the heathen, but how we can do our uttermost with a given amount of strength and money. There are in China two millions of pagans to every Protestant missionary. Of the two hundred missionary ladies in China, so many are prevented by domestic cares, by ill health, and by lack of knowledge of the language, from engaging in direct missionary work, that the proportion of heathen women to each working missionary lady is several millions. If there be no plan by which one missionary lady can give a knowledge of Christ to many thousands of heathen women, then there is no hope of the evangelization of China for generations to come.

Never were women more needy than are these Chinese women. Their homes—the homes of a third of the human race, are windowless, floorless, and ceilingless. They are very hot in summer, very cold in winter, dank and dark all the year round. They are small because of poverty; low, for safety from typhoons; unventilated, because openings would give ingress to the long hooks of thieves; densely crowded together for mutual protection; opening only on tiny courts and narrow streets, where all filth fumes, because every atom must be saved for fertilizing the rice-fields.

Villages so made up and surrounded by walls to keep out marauders, are but a few minutes' walk from each

Native Female Evangelists. 93

other, all over the land. From such a home to such a home, a woman is brought and married to a man she has never before seen, to serve a mother-in-law who is kind to her in proportion to her diligence in rearing pigs, and her aptness in bearing sons. The greater portion of the women have seen only the village in which they were born, and that into which they are married. All the world outside is as unknown to them as the planet Mars. Toward the life to come they look blankly, hoping only that their male descendants will feed their wandering spirits, after death, with earthly food.

The Chinese women are grave and patient women. Of all in the world, there are none to whom a knowledge of the way of salvation would be a more blessed boon, and none more capable of appreciating and using the gift. As hardly any Chinese women know how to read, as the old women rarely leave their villages, and the young women seldom leave their own houses, the only way to carry the gospel "to every creature" among them, is to take it by a living voice into their homes. Native sentiment, and custom which is doubtless correct, forbid the doing of this work by men. Women, and women only, can do it effectively. Native social customs permit elderly women to go freely from house to house and from village to village, and there is no limit to the number of women who may be reached and taught by them. This is scriptural, and it is so cheap that we might almost hope that with only the number of foreign workers which Christendom could send, and only that amount of money which Christian women could give, the gospel could be made known to every woman in China. The selection, training, and superintendence of native Christian women who do this work, is probably the way in which the foreign missionary lady can effect most in the work of evangelizing Asia.

A large amount of work must be done by the foreign missionary lady before the training of native female evangelists can well be begun. Usually the native Christians are scattered over a wide region, in towns and hamlets remote from each other and from the missionary residence, so that in order to become acquainted with them she is obliged to make difficult and wearisome journeys. Only in this way can she learn the exact condition of her people, and gain such familiarity with the field itself that she can definitely and wisely direct the native women when they are engaged in their work. In this way too she ascertains the needs of the masses of heathen women, and comes to know what is the kind and amount of education required by the evangelists in order to render them most useful.

When the amount to be expended is limited, it is important that much care be exercised in the selection of the women to be taught, and that they may be such as will be able to convey to others the knowledge that is given to themselves. I have found it best not to take into my class those who offer themselves as pupils; but to seek out, and invite to it, those whose character is such as to recommend them for the work. Even when the allowance given for food was so low as not to tempt the most needy to enter the class for the food's sake, some who thought the school house pleasanter than their own houses, or who had domestic troubles that they wished to get away from, or who hoped that their absence from home might bring an obdurate mother-in-law to terms, came as applicants for admission to the school. Only when thoroughly acquainted with the

Native Female Evangelists.

women invited to join the class, can we feel sure that we are spending our time and money on those who are seeking the Truth solely for the Truth's sake. We have the joy of finding many such in our classes, and such will and do remain steadfast through much hardship in the work to which they are called. Even when reasonable care is taken in the selection of the women to be trained, fully half of those who are tried are found to be incompetent for the work. Many are dismissed on account of physical weakness, or bad temper, or duplicity, or an inability to deliver the gospel message plainly. Some study a few months and then return to their homes to be more joyous and intelligent Christians all their lives; some study for years, and grow in grace in a wonderful way.

Of a hundred women admitted to my own training-school at Swatow during ten years, about one-third became capable of aptly instructing others.

There are many difficulties and dangers in the work of training native female evangelists. It is hard for us, whose social life and modes of thought are so unlike those of the Chinese, to obtain such intimate personal acquaintance with the native Christians, that we can accurately judge which of them has that style of speech and character which the Chinese themselves consider worthy of imitation. The women who go out as teachers are taken by the heathen as types of the result of a Christian education. It is therefore of the utmost importance that they should be tolerably true exponents of Christian principles and modes of life.

Though it is true that she who lives most gracefully in a mansion would be likely to live with truest dignity in a hut, the transposition would be made with much personal discomfort. So we need to be careful that our course of training does not practically unfit these women for living in the narrow and uncleanly quarters in which the masses of the people dwell. Even tastes and habits which may not in themselves be admirable, are better left unchanged if the changing of them will in any degree separate the woman from those among whom she is to work. Some of the most valuable work done by the Bible-women, is done at meal-times and in the night-time, among the women with whom they eat and lodge. No one knows better than the Chinese how to get the greatest amount of personal comfort out of the smallest amount of money. If we make sure that our native evangelists are able and faithful in making known the Word of God to those around them, we need not fear that the cleanliness which is next to godliness will not come to be prized in due time.

All this does not mean that a Bible-woman is not to be educated, but rather that she is to have that sort of education which fits her for her place. This is the work of years, both for herself and for her teacher. A purely Scriptural education does not make one less akin to any human creature.

As the Bible is the only book that the women are expected to teach, it is the only one that they study; and those in any country who have seriously set to work to master the contents of the Bible have found that they need for that purpose the whole of every day for a lifetime. The women need to be taught to use their own language with force and fluency; to read correctly, easily, and agreeably; to speak clearly, truthfully, and attractively; and to pertinently illustrate, by parable, anecdote, and proverb, the truth they communicate.

Native Female Evangelists.

They must learn the most effective manner of presenting the idea of a sole and true God, and the uselessness of idols, and the best way of removing the fear and dread of demons from ignorant and superstitious minds. Above all, they must be so taught of God that they go forth to their work knowing it to be His and theirs.

As they are to teach those who cannot read, it is desirable that they themselves should be orally instructed, and that the method of teaching them should be a constant practical exhibition of the way in which they are to teach others. They learn the Bible stories, orally taught, with great rapidity, and tell them with vivacity. It is not unusual for a woman who has never before learned to read, to become able in a single year to read the four Gospels and the Book of Acts, and to tell from memory in detail the whole life of Christ, with the miracles and parables. Some of the women become eloquent speakers, and I have seen them hold an audience of untaught women motionless and attentive for hours, even late at night and with sleeping children in their laps. The women from the Swatow school go out two and two, for three months at a time, stopping in rooms prepared for them, and connected with the chapels at the various out-stations, and from thence they go out to teach in the surrounding villages. To the nearest villages they go in the morning and return at night; in the more distant ones they stay several days, if any woman there is pleased to hear their message and will therefore give them lodging. During three months, a pair of women will thus teach in from ten to thirty different villages. At the end of two months, they return and give a report of their work, and after a week of instruction and of conference, they go out again to the same or other stations.

I visit their stations as often as possible, and never send them to any place where I have not myself been, and of which I do not myself know the condition and surroundings. Each Bible-woman receives eight shillings per month, and travelling expenses. This buys food and clothing as good as, and no better than, she would have at home. This sum merely enables the woman to leave her home and do the work. It does not pay her for the fatigue nor the obloquy she endures. She must bear that for Christ's sake, and with no earthly reward. Probably the worst methods of evangelization are those which yield worldly advantages to the evangelist and the disciple. Converts brought in through selfishness, remain selfish to the end, and transmit to their spiritual children diseases that are finally fatal to the church.

It is desirable that the Bible-women, when at the country stations, should often have encouragement and advice from the foreign missionary lady. Their work is so unlike anything that the Chinese habitually do; they meet with so many rebuffs; they are under so many temptations to lag; they find such real obstacles in the way of their usefulness, that they must have help and guidance on the spot where their work lies, from some one whose wisdom and zeal is greater than their own. They dress and live as poorly as the poor women they teach; and they endure much exposure to rain, cold, and fatigue. In a way that is unknown to all other Chinese women, they go to places distant from their own homes and dwell among strangers. They often suffer extreme hardship, but no Bible-woman has ever given up her work because it was hard. Two of the women lived through the hottest months of the year in a stable, because there were numerous inquirers at a certain place

Native Female Evangelists.

and no other lodgings than the stable to be procured. Two others were badly beaten in a certain village, and yet, before their wounds were healed, these women went back to that village to continue their work, because its welfare demanded their presence. The results of such work cannot now be accurately computed. But when all those who have gone forth bearing precious seed, come again with rejoicing, these women will also come bringing their sheaves, and we shall be amazed at the greatness of the harvest.

To sum up, the conclusions which I draw in favour of this plan of work are chiefly the following:—

Firstly, *It enables us to reach a large number of people with a very small outlay of money.*

Secondly, *It enables us to use effectively the very first fruits of our missionary labour, without being compelled to wait for a highly educated class to be raised up.* By this plan all available native talent can at once be utilized in the service of the church, and can be increased as rapidly as the church increases.

Thirdly, *This was the Saviour's own method of evangelization.* Carefully chosen, faithfully superintended, His disciples, even when they are but weak Chinese women, may go out at His behest, and teach, and come back saying, "Even the devils are subject unto us."

CHAPTER XVIII.

BIOGRAPHY OF LITTLE GALE.

WHEN little Gale was born, nobody was pleased. Girls are sometimes endured, but never welcomed, in Chinese families. The neighbours did not congratulate her mother as if a boy had been born, but politely ignored the matter, as a misfortune about which the less said the better. However, as there were already three boys and no girls in the family, she was allowed to live. She had her head shaven, except two little tufts of hair over the bumps of "sublimity"; a short sack was put on her, and she was laid in a basket that swung by a rope from a beam in the roof, and thence she looked about her world. It was a very small one. The house had three rooms—a bedroom at each end, and a middle room used for all domestic purposes. From her basket Gale could watch the pigs and fowls running about, and could see the busy people in the six-feet-wide street before the door. When she grew older, she had "the three contagious diseases," chicken-pox, small-pox, and measles, which public opinion required her mother to see that she had in her infancy. As soon as she was strong enough, with her hair braided in one strand down her back, like a boy's, with a pair of short trousers on, and with a cold, boiled sweet potato for luncheon, she went with other girls to gather dry grass and sticks to cook the family food. These daily excursions with basket and rake, by the shore and on the hills, were very pleasant. To be sure, she would get hard words and blows if she did not bring fuel to boil the pot; but the sky was blue, and the birds sang meanwhile. Sometimes she wondered if all the villages she could see around her were like the one she lived in, if all the houses were like her house, and all the people poor as she; if there was any end to the sea; how far the hills went; and if there was anything beyond the sky. But all this nobody knew. She had so much work to do, that her feet were neglected, and got so large that they began to be a disgrace to the family before they were bound. She knew the pain would be dreadful, but it was more dreadful to have her neighbours say as she passed, "There are two boats going by." So she had them bound, and had to endure the pain until it ceased. Her feet could never be straightened again, and she could not go to the hills any more, for she could not walk far. One day a foreign person came to the village. It was said that he was very wonderful, with white skin, pale eyes, and red hair. Everybody ran to look, but her feet would not go fast, and she lost the sight.

She helped her mother to spin and weave the cotton cloth for the family garments, and cook the sweet potatoes and rice for the family meals. When her father and brothers had eaten, then she and her mother ate what was left. On certain days she worshipped the little gilded images that were on the shelf for gods, opposite the main door in the house; and sometimes she went with her female relations to burn incense and gilt paper before the gods in the village temple. So she came to her fifteenth year.

Meanwhile Lim, a tradesman of Swatow, had a younger brother, We, getting near twenty, and therefore of suitable age to marry. The parents and grandparents being dead, Lim was, by immutable custom, the head of the house, and took the responsibility of the departed father towards We, demanding filial obedience in return. We had front teeth like tusks, and was stupid as well as ugly. He helped Lim in the shop. Lim's wife wanted a servant, so she persuaded her husband to send a go-between to find a wife for We.

The go-between knew all the marriageable damsels in the neighbouring villages, and began bargaining for Gale. Negotiations, carried on through the go-between by the elders of the two families, who did not know each other, resulted in a betrothal between We and Gale. The bridegroom, on hearing his fate, might have run away, as Chinese bridegrooms sometimes do. But the bride had no such resort. Should she object, there was the custom of hundreds of generations behind her, and of millions of people around her, to crush out her small voice. She had never heard of any other fate for a woman. She had no precedent which she could plead.

She would have new clothes, her hair would be done up in a close butterfly shape on her crown, she would go out of her village and see the wide world, and it would all be very amusing.

The betrothal money, equal to five pounds twelve shillings, wrapped in red silk, was carried from Lim to Gale's parents; suitable red cards expressing amity and good wishes, were exchanged; and then on a day pronounced lucky by a geomancer, Gale was taken in a closed sedan chair, with a red shawl covering her head and face, to the house of her unknown bridegroom's eldest brother. There she worshipped the household gods, and was led to her room, where her veil was removed, and she saw for the first time the man who was her husband. She saw his tusks and his stupidity, and then and there began to hate him. The next day she stood among several old female friends, and all who chose, of both sexes, came to see her, and to pass comments on her, flattering, curious, or malicious, as their dispositions might impel.

Then her life of servitude began. Lim's wife was unaccustomed to power, and having got it, she used it mercilessly. She was arrogant and contemptuous towards Gale, and made her wretched. We, too, grew more and more hateful and hated.

The next neighbour to her was her aunt, one year older than she was. She had three years before been betrothed and brought home by the parents of a young man who had been absent five years. For three years she had served the old couple, awaiting the return of her expected bridegroom. For two years nothing had been heard from him; and as he ran away when he left home, his parents did not know in what country he was. The father was sick and foolish, and the mother took care of cows for the support of the family, leaving her son's betrothed wife to take care of the sick man and the house. Gale and this girl were seen in frequent conference, from which they ceased as soon as observed; then they were met very early in the morning, in gala dress, on the road to their native village, and when asked where they were going, they said "for a pleasure-trip home." Shortly after, their shoes were found on the brink of a pool used in irrigating the rice-fields, and their lifeless bodies were taken from the bottom.

CHAPTER XIX.

THE AUTOBIOGRAPHY OF AUNT LUCK.

I WAS born at Koi Tau, a village in Po Leng. My father was a store-keeper, and I was the youngest of seven children. When I was seven years old, I was betrothed, for two pounds, to a man at Nam Leng, a village a mile from my home. I had never seen the man, nor any of his family. I took nothing from home with me but the tunic and pair of trousers which I wore. My mother and the two go-betweens, who had acted as agents in my betrothal, led me to his house and left me there. I jumped up and down, and screamed to go back with my mother. My husband's mother told me not to cry, for my home was to be with her henceforth, and my husband's grandmother carried me on her back to please and quiet me, but I kept crying more or less for years. Indeed, I never really stopped crying till I had children of my own. In the family there was my husband's grandfather, grandmother, father, mother, uncles, aunts, five brothers, and four sisters-in-law. I was told which man was to be my husband, and though he was handsome, I immediately disliked him, because he seemed so old to me, being nine years older than I.

I did not see my own mother again for three years, for she was afraid I would cry and be discontented if I saw her. I always slept with my mother-in-law, and during the day I spooled the yarn which the elder ones spun and wove into cloth. At this I worked from daylight until dark, only stopping to eat. I had plenty to eat, and was whipped only when I nodded over my spools. Once a year one of my brothers came to see if I was well. He stayed but a few minutes when he came, because it might make me homesick if he talked much with me. When I was eleven years old I went to my father's house and stayed four months, and did the same each year thereafter until I was married. I learned to spin and weave and sew and cook. All this time I never spoke to my betrothed husband, and he only spoke to me to tell me to do something. At fourteen, when his mother told me to do so, I became his wife. I cooked rice, fed the pigs, and did other work for the family.

My husband never called me by any name whatever. When he wanted me to do anything, he said, "Here, you," and of course I knew he meant me. When I was sixteen I had a little girl, and then another and another. The third I strangled when it was born, for I was frightened, and knew I should be hated for having so many girls. Then I had three boys and another girl; and when I was forty I had nine children. My husband was a good-natured man, and he was not very hard toward me. In all the forty years I lived with him, he beat me only four or five times. These were occasions when I moved too slowly in serving him, and then answered back when he scolded me. There are not ten men in a thousand in China who do not beat their wives at all.

I never believed much in the gods in the temples, and we seldom went to worship there. Once, twice, and sometimes three times in a month, I and my husband, and children, with many others, used to go on fixed days to the tops of the mountains, and worship the heavens and the earth. Sometimes it was the moon we went to worship, sometimes the sun, sometimes the thunder-god. Sometimes we went to one peak, sometimes to another; and in the course of years, we went to nearly all the high peaks in and around our district. We spent from ten shillings to two pounds each time on our offerings. Sometimes my husband sold products of the farm, and sometimes I sold one of my fat pigs to get the money. We took rice, pork, tea, cakes, fruit, sugar, pies, everything that is nice to eat, and spread it out invitingly on the rocks, and burned incense and mock money. Immense centipedes, sent by the demons to see what was brought, and how many people came to worship, crawled out of the rocks and around the offerings and back into their holes again.

One by one the elders of our family, and all but three of my children, died. When I was fifty-four, that is ten years ago, my husband died also. After that I spent more time than ever worshipping upon the mountains, but I got sick and had no strength. My nephew, Leng, who had heard the True Doctrine, used to come often to see me, and tell me that there was only one God, and He was everywhere; that He made the sun to rise, the moon to change, the wind to blow, the rain to fall, and all that is. Little by little I believed what he said. As soon as I believed, I destroyed the censers we used in worshipping false gods. My sons saw me taking them out of the house, and asked me if I was not afraid to do it; but I told them that what I had myself set up I could myself take down, and they said no more. Then

I prayed earnestly that I might have strength given me to come and be baptized; and when the next communion season came, I told Leng I was coming with him to Swatow. At that time Leng was the only Christian in Po Leng, and his mother and wife beat him for worshipping God, and their neighbours applauded them. Leng said I was too weak, and must not think of coming to Swatow; but I got up off my bed, and walked very slowly the whole forty miles, and when I got here, the people said a dead woman had come.

Since then I have been in all the Po Leng villages speaking the gospel, and can walk fifteen or twenty miles a day. Nobody dares molest me when I speak of God, and those who do not believe keep silent and listen.

CHAPTER XX.

THE STORY OF SPEED AND THE BAMBOO DRAGON.

SPEED is the daughter of one of the completest Christians and best preachers that the Chinese church has possessed. From her father she has inherited a rare aptness to teach, and I have seen her hold the attention of a congregation of heathen women for hours at a time. Being under thirty years old, she is too young to do village-work as a Bible-woman; but she goes to the country stations, speaking effectively to the women who gather at the chapels, and she assists in teaching the women who are learning to read. She has singular tact in showing the other women how to narrate a Bible story. Chinese children are apparently much younger than English children of the same age.

SPEED'S STORY.

My home is twenty miles north from Swatow, and at the time when my father became a Christian I had never seen a foreigner. My father had been a man with many friends. He had such a happy style of setting the truth before people, and was so curiously wise in discerning ways in which a point could be gained, that many people came to him for advice, and generally went away convinced that his advice was worth following. He was

Speed and the Bamboo Dragon. 109

skilful in the settlement of disputes and in reconciling those at variance. He was much beloved until he became a Christian. I was a very little girl then, but I remember the disquiet with which I saw my father losing the affection and esteem of others on account of his new religion. He no sooner believed in Jesus than he became an incessant preacher of Him to others. He would talk of God to any one who happened to be walking along the street with him; he pestered the neighbours by preaching at his own door at twilight; he would sit by the roadside, or in any shed, till late into the night expounding the doctrine; he would follow and exhort people so persistently, that they used in our neighbourhood to call me "God's child" in derision.

When I was thirteen years old, my father wished to come to Swatow to join the church. We had an orange-garden, on which we depended for the support of the family, and it had to be watched constantly to protect the fruit from thieves. It was a mile from our house, and my father took great care of it. As I was the only child, and loved my father greatly, I was almost always with him there. There was a little straw hut to sleep in at night, and a close hedge all round the garden. My father told me that I must watch the garden while he was gone, and that would be for three days. I was terrified at this, for two reasons. One was that I greatly feared to stay alone in the garden; and the other was that the neighbours had said that any one who went and joined himself to the missionaries would never come back. He would have his heart and eyeballs taken out and made into a medicine, which the missionaries sold for a great price to their foreign countrymen. My father saw that I was troubled, and told me that I might have one of the neighbour's children to stay with me at the garden. I thought the matter over and decided that I would watch alone. If thieves should not come, then there would be no need of help; if thieves should come, then the other child would be frightened and cry out, and the thieves would discover by the voices that there were only children there, and would rob the garden. I, alone, would keep silent, and would strike together two pieces of broken bowl, and throw stones toward all the gates, and the thieves would think that there was a grown person with weapons there, and would run away. So I left my mother guarding the house, and took food with me and went to the garden, which was on the road to Swatow. It was Saturday, and my father said he would be back on Monday. To me it seemed as if he had said he would be back in three years. I wondered in my heart whether I should ever see him again, and then wondered if when he came back he would see me again; but I did not speak a word of what I thought. I laid broken tiles before all the places where the thieves were likely to come in, so that I could hear a rattling if any one stepped on them, and gathered little heaps of stones to throw, and put some broken crockery beside me, and I slept unmolested in the hut. On Monday I made a little hole in the hedge toward the Swatow road, and watched all day for the coming of my father. As it grew late in the afternoon, I began to cry, and at dark I could endure it no longer. I left the garden to its fate and ran home, careful that no one should see me and thus know that the garden was unwatched. I threw myself into my mother's lap, saying, "Father has not come, and what the neighbours say about the foreigners is true then." But in a few minutes my father came; and then I

Speed and the Bamboo Dragon.

thought, "If I had only stayed in the garden a little longer, he would have praised me; now he will be displeased that I have left the garden unwatched." But he did not reprove me by a single word, and we went back to the garden together, and found all safe.

After this, as my father kept on preaching, my mother and several of our neighbours believed. There was a woman living near us who could read and write, and was expert in cutting figures and flowers from red paper, and was a popular talker behind shadow-pictures. This caused her to be much liked in the community. My father went to her, and told her about the importance of having no god but God, and she was enraged that one who did not know how to read should come to teach her who was well known as a scholar. Our former friends took her part, and my father was more derided than ever. But he kept on arguing with her, and finally she sent her son to Swatow to see the missionaries, and hear what they said. She is now the Bible-woman Snow, and her son is the preacher Po San.

I was baptized when I was fourteen. I learned to read in the mission-school. Before I went to school I wished to have my feet bound that I might be like other girls, but my father told me that if I insisted on having my feet bound, my hands should be bound also. After I went to school I was very glad that my feet were free, and now my husband approves of feet naturally shaped. I often go to visit Christian women in different villages, and I often speak of the true God to those who have not before been taught. A few weeks ago I was at Am Choi, and a large bamboo dragon, such as is worshipped in some places, floated down the river and lodged on the bank, with its mouth toward the village.

It had been made from bamboo twigs contributed by many people, and had an immense snout and glaring eyes, and was painted in gorgeous colours, and was very hideous. Soothsayers were frequently consulted in regard to it, and when they said it wanted to be in the water, it was lowered reverently into the river; and when it wished to be on land, it was lifted into a temple and served devoutly with many offerings and prostrations. One night the current carried the dragon away to Am Choi, where it filled all the inhabitants with terror. It was thought that it bred pestilence, and that sickness would prevail in its neighbourhood. The people told me what harm the dragon did among them, and one of the women led me to go and take a peep at the dreadful thing. The friends of the sick ones were there, making propitiatory offerings, throwing the offerings away after the ceremony of presenting them, instead of eating them as they would eat offerings to beneficent deities. No one dared to touch the dragon, nor to push it off the bank. It was thought that the only safe measure was to bring to it pork, ducks, and fruit, and that by such presents, combined with worship, it might be induced to refrain from producing disease. I told the woman who had brought me to see the dragon that there is but one true God, who is invisible, and who keeps those who serve Him from the power of all dragons and evil spirits of every kind. And then after praying to Him, the Almighty One, I punched holes in the dragon with my umbrella, and pushed it off the shore. All the bystanders were amazed, and many came afterward to me that I might tell them about the God who protected me,

CHAPTER XXI.

GOLD GETTER.

THIS woman, who was forty-two years old, and who did not previously know a letter, learned in ten months to read fluently a hundred hymns, the whole of the four Gospels, and the book of Acts, and to tell from memory nearly all she had read.

Gold Getter's Story.

I was the second child and eldest daughter in a family of many children. My elder brother had been named Coming Wealth, and I was called Gold Getter, through a poetic idea that a fine girl is worth two hundred pounds of betrothal money. We lived in a hamlet of about four hundred people. The place was so small that it was quiet, and there were only two theatrical performances a year, one in the first and one in the twelfth month. A company of actors was brought by the head men of the village; a platform, with a roof over it, was put up in an open space, and some mats with the red boxes holding the actors' costumes formed the sides and back of the theatre. The front was left open toward the area for spectators. The play continued through an afternoon and the following night, and was performed for the amusement of the gods, who were previously consulted as to the time when they could conveniently attend.

Although the plays were primarily for the pleasure of the gods, all the people of the village, and many from neighbouring villages, came to look on. A performance cost from thirty shillings to four pounds, according to the skill of the actors and the magnificence of the costumes exhibited. It was paid for by an assessment upon all the men and married women in the village. Boys, though only a few days old, paid a tax, but unmarried girls were not counted. The assessment often amounted to three-halfpence or twopence for each member of a family.

In our hamlet there was no temple, but just outside the village there was a shrine, where the chief god of the vicinity was supposed to dwell. There was no image, but only an incense-urn set up on some stones, with a little roof over it. I never heard what this god was, but every place has a peculiar god. Besides this there was the god of the kitchen, and several other gods that we worshipped at the new and the full moon, at the eight festivals, and at other times, so that we worshipped as many as forty times a year. My mother taught me how to worship the gods when I was very young, first making me stand at her side to see how she did it, and then having me do as she had done.

When I was married I went to live at Silver Plains, a city of twenty thousand people. There were as many as thirty or forty large temples, with many gods in them, and there were many rich and powerful families living there. The family into which I was married was rich, and at that time I lived very comfortably. My husband was the youngest of six brothers, and was twenty-nine years old. Soon after my marriage there were clan feuds in Silver Plains, and at one time the people on one

Gold Getter. 115

side of our street were at war with those on the other side, so that we kept our doors barricaded, and could not safely go out. These feuds wasted the family property, and sickness wasted the household. I had ten children, seven boys and three girls, but only one son and one daughter lived. My husband was injured in a fight between two parties in our own clan, and on consulting a spirit-medium in regard to a remedy for his wounds, he was told that he would never get well unless he at once went abroad. He went, with only four shillings to meet expenses, and I have never since heard of him.

Eight years ago a woman, who was a stranger to me, came as the agent of an acquaintance to negotiate for the betrothal of my daughter to a young man in another village. This woman told me about a true God, and told me where to go to hear the True Doctrine, in the District City, a league away. After that I went twice to the chapel to which she had directed me, but as it happened to be on other days than Sunday, and as I did not find the woman I knew there, I did not go in. After my daughter was married, I lived alone with my little son in a room which I hired for eight shillings a year, and supported myself by weaving cotton cloth for a penny a yard, the yarn furnished. In this way I earned on an average threepence a day.

Three years ago I became acquainted with a church member, who told me when Sunday came, and I again went to the chapel, taking my son with me. I used to go in all sorts of weather, and my neighbours derided me for lack of thrift, saying that by ceasing to work, paying my boat-fare, and spoiling my clothes in the rain, I lost two days' earnings in that one day. But I kept on, and heard the preaching at the chapel for five months, and then I was baptized.

My son will not go to theatres, even when his playmates try hard to induce him; and when I go out teaching the gospel, he tries to preach too. When I was last at my native village, the women there said if I would come and teach them about the true God, they would surely believe. There are many tens of hamlets among the hills where I could go, as my feet are not bound, and I think many women there would believe the True Doctrine if they heard it.

CHAPTER XXII.

KEEPSAKE.

MY name is Keepsake. I am fifty-four years old, and have been a Bible-woman four years. I have now no near relative but the Lord, and have nothing to do but His work. If I had accepted the gospel when He first sent it to me thirty years ago, perhaps I might have kept much that I then had and loved; but I would not heed His message till He chastened me by taking away the earthly things to which my heart clung.

My father was a fish-merchant, and did an extensive business. He died when I was three years old. I had five brothers and a sister, and as I was much younger than any of them, I was a pet in the family. My eldest brother studied for a literary degree, but as he was fonder of making pictures than of reading, he failed to pass his examination. My second brother was a most filial son. When my mother entered a room in which he was sitting, he would immediately rise, and remain standing so long as she was there. He was also very talented. He began to attend the examinations when he was only fourteen years old, and when he was eighteen he got a degree. Then he taught and studied for a higher degree; but before he attained it he died, at the age of twenty-five. My younger brothers tilled our land. Though there were two scholars in our family, I was never taught to read. Girls are not taught to read unless they are the only children, and their fathers may then teach them for pleasure.

My mother was forty-four years older than I, and she was always very tender toward me. I had my feet bound when I was thirteen years old; but when they ached in the night, my mother would tell me to loosen the bandages. Bound feet ache worse when they are still.

When I was fourteen years old, I was betrothed to a young man at the city of Chung Lim, a league from my home. An old neighbour acted as go-between, and went to and fro between the families, till all the preliminaries were settled. My future mother-in-law was very particular in previously ascertaining whether I would bring good fortune to her household. After learning the year, month, day, and hour of my birth, she consulted a blind fortune-teller, and got a favourable answer; then she worshipped before her family gods, tossing up a split bamboo-root till it fell so as to give an auspicious omen; then she made offerings to the gods in the temple, and got from their interpreter a sign of acquiescence. After that, on a day chosen as lucky, the go-between brought three pounds done up in red paper, and my mother received it. With that the bargain was concluded, and could not be broken by any of the persons involved. I was not consulted in the matter, and no one told me anything about it; but I overheard what was said, and knew very well what was going on, though I dared not ask any questions. When I was seventeen, a lucky day was fixed upon, three pounds more were paid to my mother, and I was carried to my mother-in-law's house. My mother had been busy for some months in preparing my wedding outfit. It consisted of two wash-tubs, two trunks, two strong cloth bags for clothing, two large red lanterns, a thick cotton coverlet, a pillow, sixty garments for summer and winter wear, embroidered shoes, hair ornaments of silver washed with gold, bracelets, and earrings. My jewellery was worth four pounds, and my outfit altogether cost over twelve pounds. I have still the coverlet and one tunic which my mother then gave me. The jewellery I have given to my daughter, except a pair of bracelets which were torn off my wrists the day that we Christians were attacked and beaten by a mob, in the chapel at Chung Lim.

If people are very poor, they give their daughters only a suit or two of clothing when they are married. If they are rich they give them much more than the amount of the betrothal money. I knew a man who gave his daughter a wedding outfit worth two hundred pounds, and it included a rice-field.

I was troubled about going away from home, and anxious lest I should be unable to perform the duties of a daughter-in-law, and I did not look upon my new garments with pleasure. But all girls have to be married, and of course I must be. The day before my marriage, my mother gathered twelve kinds of flowers, and steeped them in water, and the next morning I was washed in this water, and dressed in an entire suit of new clothing, with a fine outer garment that my mother-in-law had hired from a wealthy official, and sent for the occasion. I was then put into a sedan-chair, and as it was lifted up, my mother took water in which green peas had been steeped and threw it on the top of the chair, for good luck. Only the go-between went with me to my mother-in-law's house. The go-between stayed three days and waited upon me, then she went home. She received eight shillings from my husband's mother, and four shillings from my mother, for the performance of her part in the transaction.

After three days, my mother sent my nephew to bring me a bottle of hair-oil, and to inquire after me. At the end of a month, he came again, and brought me an artificial flower, and a basket of boiled rice. At the end of four months, my mother sent a sedan-chair for me, and I went and ate breakfast with her. It is not the custom for a mother to visit her married daughter until the latter has had children; and then the mother-in-law must go and invite the mother to come.

My husband was seven years older than I, and his elder brother's wife had already been brought home. The house had three bedrooms; one for the mother, one for the older brother and his wife, and one for my husband and myself. There was, besides, a common kitchen, and a living-room. My husband's father was dead. Like all daughters-in-law, I cooked, sewed, washed, wove, and fed pigs. I had four children, two boys and two girls; but one boy and one girl died when very young. My mother-in-law also died when I was twenty-one.

Some thirty years ago my youngest brother heard a missionary preach, and became a Christian. My brother used to come and tell me about God, and would explain the True Doctrine to me until the perspiration would run down his cheeks, through his exertions in making me understand. He came again and again; but though I saw that what he said must be true, my heart clung to the old idols, and I wanted to adhere to the customs followed by my friends. My head received the truth, but my heart rejected it. God has many ways of making people repent. Had my husband prospered in business I should never have turned to the Lord.

When I was thirty-four years old, my husband went with a cargo of goods to Siam; and there he took to smoking opium, lost money rapidly, and never came back any more. I diligently made offerings to the gods, and every year spent as much as two pounds in mock money and incense to be burned before them. I consulted fortune-tellers to inquire when a letter or money would come from my husband, and would often get the answer for a certain day. Then I would sit in the door and watch for the coming of the letter; and when any one that looked like a letter-carrier approached, my heart would beat fast; and when I found there was no letter for me, I would go in and cry. After I had spent much devotion and money on the gods, and found that they always disappointed me, I began to think my brother's God might be better. I went to him and said, " Brother, hereafter I am going to worship God; but as there are so many who will oppose and despise me, I will only worship Him secretly." My brother told me that every one who belonged to Christ must confess Him before men. I went home and thought it over, and began to go on Sundays to worship with the few Christians at Chung Lim. My son was so vexed when he knew that I meant to be a Christian, that he cried; and my sister-in-law, who had before been very friendly with me, hated me, and locked the door so that I could not get in when I came from the chapel. It was very troublesome, indeed, being a Christian.

When my son was eighteen years old, he went to Siam to search for his father, hoping to induce him to give up opium. The next year, when I was forty-one, I came with some of the brethren and sisters from Chung Lim to Swatow, to be baptized. I had to come secretly; and I sent my extra clothing, with rice and cash for the journey, to the chapel on the previous evening; and early in the morning I came out and joined the Christian company on the road. Before I got back to Chung Lim, my sister-in-law went to three of the four chief men of our clan and told them what I had done; and they agreed to wait on the brink of the river for me, and catch me as I was crossing, and push me into the river bottom and keep me there till I died. But she went last to the head of the clan, and though the reasons she gave for my having gone to Swatow were too bad to be spoken, he told her that the foreign teachers were powerful, and that she might get herself into serious trouble by killing a Christian; so my life was saved. When I got home, she reviled me, but nothing more. She would never let me preach the gospel in our house, nor let any one who believed in it come to visit me. When I am sick, my daughter, who is married into a family that lives but a few streets off, and whose mother-in-law is very obliging, comes and takes care of me.

My son went into business in Siam, and then came up to Hong Kong. From there he sent me four pounds, and a message asking my pardon for his lack of filial love in not coming to see me; but his ship was going back at once to Siam, and he must go with it. When only one day out from Hong Kong, the ship was wrecked, and all on board were lost.

When I heard this news, I did not cry, except in secret; for I feared that the heathen around me would say that my God was not good. I thought, too, that I must set the weak Christians an example of submission to the will of God. I have felt that my grief was greater than I could bear; but I have kept it shut up in my heart, and have never, until to-day, told any one how great it was.

I have nothing now to rest my heart upon but the hope of heaven. I have been deeply troubled; but without the trouble I should not have been saved. I am strong, and have perhaps many years to live; and if I can but lead many to believe in the Lord, that will be joy enough for me here.

CHAPTER XXIII.

ORCHID LOSES SEVEN-TENTHS OF HER SORROW.

MY name is Orchid. I am twenty-eight years old, and have been a Christian one year. My home is at White Pagoda, and I have lived there with my mother-in-law ever since I was two months old. My father was a farmer, and could have taken care of me; but shortly after my birth a blind fortune-teller came along and told my mother that my brother, who was two years older than I, would die unless I was removed from the family. Blind fortune-tellers are to be found everywhere. They travel about, led by a child that can see, beating a little gong to let people know they are passing. Those who wish to consult the fortune-teller call him to their door, tell him the year, month, day, and hour of their birth, and he makes a calculation of times, and tells them what is going to happen. Those who are sick, ask him when they will get well; those who have absent relatives inquire when letters or money will come from abroad; those who are going on a journey seek a lucky day for starting; and those who wish to know what is going to happen to their children, call him to predict their fates. He gives a few words of advice to the person concerned, is paid three-tenths of a halfpenny for his services, and goes on his way.

It was in this way that my parents learned that they

ought to part with me. They were very sorry to have me go, but as a boy is of so much greater value than a girl, they would not risk my brother's life by keeping me. They gave me to an acquaintance at White Pagoda, who had just lost a young child, and she brought me up as the future wife of her youngest son, then five years old. As such very little girls are worth nothing, and as the bargain must be closed by money, she paid my mother one penny for me, and I became hers. She had had twelve children in all, but my husband was the only survivor. Her husband smoked opium, and spent the money his children earned, so that one of his sons had hanged himself in despair.

My mother-in-law always gave me the best she had, but that was not much. I grew strong and large, and when I was eight years old I could cook, spin, plant rice, and help to turn the pump with which the rice-field was watered. When I was fifteen, on a day chosen as lucky, I had the god of the bedstead set up in a room of my own, and lived with my husband. After some years I had two sons. My father-in-law died; and then we found that the land on which our house was built belonged to some one else. The owner tore it down and made a rice-drying place where it stood. We then mortgaged our only field, for eight pounds, and with this money built two houses, which fell down soon after in a season of heavy rain.

Three years ago, a man in our village became a Christian: soon after that two Bible-women came to stop at his house. My mother-in-law and I used to take the children in the evening and go to hear them talk. My husband heard too, and we all believed at the same time. My mother-in-law went one Sunday morning five miles to Linden Chapel, and when she came back at night she went straight to the god of the bedstead, and taking it out of doors threw it away. Afterward the Bible-woman named Love came to the house, and after engaging in prayer took down the only other idol in the house, the one we had inherited from our ancestors, and put it with its fixtures in a basket, which my mother-in-law carried and threw into the river.

When my own father and mother heard that I had become a Christian, they were very much distressed; my mother cried, and my father could not eat for four days. My aunt came to tell me how displeased they were, and that they wished me to put away this new religion, but I told her to say that anything else they might ask of me I could do, but that this religion was something that could not be put away.

Last year my husband, finding the times hard, and hoping to earn something abroad, went to Manilla. Before he went, he did not call a fortune-teller to find a lucky day, and did not go to the temple to get a bag of incense ashes to wear as a charm on his breast, as he would have done had he not been a Christian; but we knelt down, with the children, and asked God to take care of us while he was gone, and bless him while away, and bring him safely back.

Last month my eldest son, eleven years old, was baptized. I did not know it beforehand, though four months previously he had told me he wished to join the church. He did not tell me, because he was afraid the brethren would not receive him. I was surprised, and thanked God, when I saw him at the place of baptism.

My youngest son is five years old, and my mother-in-

Orchid loses Seven-tenths of her Sorrow.

law takes care of him while I am away from home. We have a house of one room, which is mortgaged for two pounds. My husband lately sent home two pounds; but it was all used in paying my father-in-law's debts.

I have been sorrowful from my childhood up. I have never known a time when I had not reason for great anxiety. But during the past year, though my earthly circumstances remain the same, I have been almost happy. I know that there is a Saviour and a heaven, and that has taken away seven-tenths of the weight of my troubles.

CHAPTER XXIV.

LOVE'S PURPOSES.

I WAS born at the village of Lo Poi, thirty-one years ago. My father died just before I was born, but I had elder brothers who helped my mother in the support of the family. When I was sixteen years old I was married into the village of Kam E, a league away from my home. My mother got six pounds at my betrothal, and at my marriage two hundred pounds of pastry and confectionery, worth four pounds more. People now pay almost double what they then did for their daughters-in-law. I do not know whether it is because money is more plentiful or because girls are more scarce.

My husband was the second of five sons, and sixteen years older than I. I neither liked or disliked him at first. My mother-in-law was kind to me, and my sisters-in-law friendly. At first my husband seldom said anything to me except to tell me to do things about the house. After we got acquainted, we talked together in private, but never when any one saw us. In this country young married people do not speak to each other in the presence of the husband's father and mother, nor of any of the older members of the family. We often talked together in our own room about family and neighbourhood affairs.

My first child was a boy, but he died when only a few

days old, and I adopted a little girl two years old and brought her up in his stead. The following year my only other child, my son Perfection, was born.

At first my husband was moral, but he took suddenly to gambling, and kept at it for six years. He lost much money, got into debt, and was very bad-tempered. About seven years ago, Silver Flower, who is my aunt by marriage, became a Christian. She came to me and told me about the true God, but there was no one else in our village who believed as she did, and every one derided her religion, and disliked her for teaching it. I had spent much time with her before, but for three years after she became a Christian I never went to her house, and seldom spoke to her. But one night I dreamed a curious dream. I thought that the sky was all on fire, and people everywhere were weeping and wailing. I got up and went out of our door, and there stood Aunt Silver Flower, looking up calmly into the sky, and her garments were glistening and beautiful. I knelt down by her and took hold of the hem of her garment and said, "What shall I do to be saved?" Then there was a crash, and I woke. After that, I kept wondering at my having had such a dream, and was so troubled in my mind that at last I went and told it to Aunt Silver Flower. She said that there would come a day when God would judge the world, and it would all be burned up. She talked much about the True Doctrine, and I told my husband all that she said. He said that he would himself go to the chapel in the district city ten miles off, and see whether what was taught there was good or bad. He went two Sundays, and then said that I could go too if I wished. He soon stopped gambling and changed into another man. He had been very

K

bad-tempered while he gambled, but after he became a Christian he became inexpressibly good. After five months he went secretly away to Singapore. He owed twelve pounds in Kam E, and he knew that if I thought he was going away I would cry, and his creditors would find out that he was going and would prevent him. So he went without telling me, but he soon wrote back and let me know where he was. I kept on going to the chapel, and four years ago I was baptized. After that I learned to read the gospel, and I have now been to seventy villages with the Lord's message. I do not know how many women have believed it. I am sure of only a very few who have become Christians because of my words.

My daughter is now twelve years old, and is in school. I shall betroth her to no one but a Christian, and shall never have her feet bound. It is difficult to find a desirable husband for her. I cannot let her go far from our home, for I must see her often. She must be married to some one who has land or a trade, that she and her children may have food; and to some one whose mother will treat her kindly. It is hard to find all that is essential in one family. When Christians are more numerous the duty of Christian parents to their daughters will be more easily performed.

My son is now nine years old, and is in school. He has applied for baptism.

My husband gets twenty-five shillings a month now in Singapore, and last year he sent home eight pounds. I have just paid the last of his debt, and he says he will soon come home. I pray every day for him, and that he may soon come back. I want him to come, and learn to preach. He can read quite well now, and he himself writes all the letters he sends me. When he comes back I shall still be a Bible-woman. If I lived at home with my husband I could still teach our relatives and neighbours, but I could not teach nearly so many people as I now do. I should like my husband to come and be a preacher, and then I should be wholly happy. I do not plan much for my future, but trust to God to order it all aright for me.

CHAPTER XXV

ONE NIGHT'S WORK.

MY name is Minute. I am now forty-five years old, and my son is eleven. I was born on the border of the Hakka country. The people in the villages west of us all spoke the Hakka language, and those in the villages east of us all spoke the Tie Chiu. These dialects are so different that a person who knows only one cannot understand what is said in the other. I learned both in my childhood, and can now speak them with equal ease. My father owned land, and we lived comfortably. Indeed my lot has been a pleasant one compared with that of other women, for though I have never been very happy, neither have I been very miserable. Hakka women do not have their feet bound. They work in the fields, and are more strong and comfortable than women who work indoors with crippled feet. They do not depend on the gods very much either, and only worship them four times a year.

I was the eldest, in a family of five children; was betrothed when I was fifteen, and married when I was seventeen years old. My husband's father was dead, and there were four sisters-in-law of us, who lived with our mother-in-law. After a few years my husband died, leaving me with one son. We had two acres of land,

and a room in the house, as our share of the ancestral property, and lived much as our neighbours did.

Two years ago there was no Christian in our village except my nephew Gek. He had heard the gospel at Linden Chapel, seven miles away, and always went there on Sundays. He often said to me that I ought to worship God, but I did not know who God was, and did not wish to be bothered with any new doctrines. One day two Bible-women came to our village, and sat in Gek's house and talked, and many women went to hear them. I was interested in what they said, but their words did not really enter my mind, nor reach my heart. When it grew late, they said that if we would like to hear more they would stay all night, and I invited them to sleep with me. After we had gone to bed, they talked till nearly morning. They told me who God was, and what He did, and about heaven, and the Lord. I shall never forget what they said that night. I believed it; and my son, nine years old, heard all they said, and believed also. Afterward he kept saying to me, "Mother, let us be Christians."

The chapel was so far away that I could not go to it on Sundays, but I joined the Bible-women and came by boat to Swatow one time. On the way back I passed my mother's house and stopped to see her, and she was very angry about my having been to Swatow. She said, "Why should you, who have enough to eat, and are a woman of good reputation, go wandering off to distant towns as if you were a beggar or worse? Who has deluded you into such conduct?" I told her that I went to get something that I wanted more than anything else, and that I should try to obtain at any cost. But my mother would not understand me, and was never pacified until my brother came and saw the women's school, and went back and told her that the people here were eminently respectable, and that the doctrine taught was righteous.

There are now ten Christians in my village, and one of them is my sister-in-law. My mother-in-law has just died, a believer.

CHAPTER XXVI.

THE HERB THAT GREW ON A PIRATE ISLAND.

MY parents lived in one of a cluster of eighteen villages. My father was wealthy, and in my childhood I was well cared for. The only real suffering I remember having endured in those days was that of having my feet bound, when I was fourteen years old.

Now that I have come to know the True Doctrine, I know that foot-binding is a very wicked and injurious custom. God gave us our eyes and hands and feet as implements with which to do His work, and we are very wicked when we destroy any of them. In remodelling our feet, we declare that the pattern by which He makes feet does not suit us, and that we ourselves can improve His handiwork. But women cannot be natural-footed, unless men are taught that such women are desirable for wives.

I was not to have been married until I was twenty, but there was a feud between the villages, five small ones uniting against our large one, and the consequent insecurity of life and property, made my parents consent to my leaving them when I was eighteen. My new home was on the island of Sun Buc, across a strait from the eighteen villages. The people of this island were so turbulent, that when there was a settlement of the boundary line between the two districts on the opposite sides of the bay, neither magistrate wanted Sun Bue under his control, and each tried to palm it off on the other. But they put chaff on the water at the head of the bay at full tide, and when at the ebb it floated northward of Sun Bue, the magistrate of the southern district had to take the island under his government. The island had only one village upon it, and the people were too few and weak to dare to be very bad. But the coves around the island harboured pirate boats, that came out to attack and plunder all boats with weaker crews that ran between the cities above and below. They sold the goods and held the passengers for ransom. The sums received for the ransom of a prisoner varied with his ability to pay. I did not hear of any one for whom the pirates got over forty pounds.

The family into which I was married was a large one, and there were twenty people who ate in our house. I and my sister-in-law had all the cooking to do, and as I had never worked much in my father's house, it was at first very hard for me. My sister-in-law and I took turns in getting up before daylight to pound the husks off the rice for the day's consumption. We had also the pigs and ducks to feed, all the water to carry, and the washing to do. My husband was a fisherman. I had three sons and six daughters, but as no one kept more than three girls, I cast away three of mine. I did not then know, as I now do, that infanticide is a great sin. One of my sons died, and my three daughters are now grown up and married. I have not yet secured wives for my two living sons. The pirate boats were dispersed, and the island made inoffensive, when General Pang came into power some years since.

Five years ago, when I was forty-five years old, a

The Herb that Grew on a Pirate Island. 137

missionary lady came to Sun Bue, and sat down and talked with the women in my neighbour's house. I went and heard what she said, and after she went away I asked my sister-in-law where she thought the place could be where there was no sickness nor weeping. She said she did not well know, but she thought it was somewhere in Hades. Then a Bible-woman came and taught us more, and I took the charms off the door-posts of our house, and off my sons' necks, and ceased to trust in idols. The Bible-woman stayed some days, and slept with my sister-in-law, but then some of the neighbours drove her away, and said that if we let any more heresy-teaching women come and lodge in our house, they would tear it down. But my husband and sons and sister-in-law and I prayed together to the true God every day, with the doors shut. After awhile the neighbours let the Bible-woman come back, and made no more violent objection to her teaching in the village. Now all there have heard the gospel, though only a few have believed it.

CHAPTER XXVII.

TAPESTRY.

THE village in which I was born was one of many on the north bank of the Crooked River. I suppose there were fifty villages within a circle having a radius of three miles. These villages were continually engaged in feuds. They were so from times long before I was born, until General Pang came into power, and he reduced the country to subjection and order. Sometimes the feud was between clan and clan, sometimes between village and village, and sometimes between different families in the same village. The weak gave their adherence to the more powerful, and depended on them for protection. When the feud was between clan and clan it was less disastrous, for then there was a greater number on one side, and some of the people could safely engage in peaceful occupation. But when it was between village and village it was very distressing to all concerned. The unripe grain would be cut down, the grown sugar-cane destroyed, the sweet-potatoes and peanuts pulled up by enemies in the night, and nothing was safe. In those days people did not dare go outside the village after nightfall for fear of being killed or kidnapped. The highways were unsafe both for travellers and for goods. My own grandfather had owned much land, but was compelled to sell it to ransom my father, who had been kidnapped and taken to a powerful village of another clan.

It was because of these feuds that my family was poor when I was born. I was the oldest child and only daughter, and was beloved by my parents. My mother betrothed me when I was about ten years old to a boy of my own age in a neighbouring village. When I was fourteen my mother died, and although the time for my marriage had not arrived, my future mother-in-law at once took me to her own house. This mother-in-law was of a cruel disposition, and very oppressive to her sons' wives. Her eldest son, an adopted one, had taken his wife and gone to live in another house; her second son had a wife, nineteen years old, in the house; and I was to be the third son's wife. My sister-in-law seldom saw her husband, and I never saw my betrothed. I do not even now know whether he was short or tall. My sister-in-law and I slept in the same room with our mother-in-law, and lived in the back part of a house whose front was a shop where the men lived and transacted business. We cooked the meals, and a small boy came and took them to the room where the men ate, while we ate by ourselves in the women's apartments. Shortly after I went to this house my sister-in-law told me that she intended to kill herself, and I soon agreed to join her in suicide. This is not an uncommon thing for unhappy daughters-in-law to do. In the village of Sieh Tie, near ours, there were seven girls who made a compact to drown themselves together. The time fixed upon was noonday, and the rendezvous a lone spot on the bank of the river. It happened that four of the girls were employed in preparing the family meal, and could not go at the set time. The other three bound their wrists together, with the youngest, who was only fourteen years old, in the middle, and thus threw themselves into the river, where their bodies were afterwards found. At Sin Hu three girls, two of whom were lately married, also drowned themselves together. They were heard running on the bank, and were seen by fishermen when they jumped into the river, but were supposed to be ghosts until some one argued that the footsteps of ghosts did not resound, nor did ghosts splash the water when descending into it.

One day, when our mother-in-law was away, my sister-in-law got a rope and fastened it over a beam, and made all ready for our hanging ourselves. But when she got upon the bedstead to try the noose I was terribly frightened, and begged her to desist, saying that if she did it first I should be so horrified that I could not follow her. She then said she would wait till another day, and that as I had a father who loved me and might help me, I had better live. Shortly after, my father sent for me to come home on a visit, and as my mother-in-law did not think it wise to offend him, she let me go. Two months later my sister-in-law hung herself, and in the disgrace and trouble that followed, I was left at my father's for some time. There was one woman in our village whose daughter-in-law hung herself, and when the mother-in-law came in and found her thus, she, fearing the demands that would be made upon her by the girl's parents, got another rope at once, and hanged herself beside her daughter-in-law. There could be then no exactions by the friends of either party, for each had harmed the other to the same degree.

My mother-in-law did not hang herself; but fearing that I also might do her some harm, she decided to marry me off. She got for me as much as she had previously paid for me, about eight pounds. Wives are much dearer now than they were then, and one cannot be got in our village for less than fourteen pounds of betrothal money. I was then nearly seventeen years old. I was glad to go from a husband who was invisible, and a mother-in-law who was hateful, to another house My second mother-in-law was kind, and my husband was an upright and affectionate man. He was twelve years older than I, and was engaged in business. I had three children, and my husband was fond of them, good to me, and very filial to his old mother.

Ten years ago, when I was twenty-five, General Pang subdued the clans, burned the houses of those who would not desist from feuds, and severely punished many as a warning to the rest. As my husband had been engaged in supplying the combatants with powder and shot, and as his neighbours chose to put him forward to receive the punishment that must be dealt out to some one in our village, and as he had not money with which to pay a fine, he fled to Singapore, whereupon General Pang banished him for twelve years. When he went he was greatly grieved at parting with the children, and knelt down and did obeisance to his mother. My youngest child was ten months old when he went. He has been gone nine years. I wish he could secretly come and see me and the children, and then go back undiscovered by his enemies. Some, who were banished and who returned too soon, have been caught and beheaded.

Three years ago I was at the district city to buy flax, and met an acquaintance who was going to the chapel, and who asked me to go with her. I went, and was much pleased with the doctrine I heard there, but after

I got home my neighbours derided me for having been there, and I did not go again. Afterward a chapel was opened a league from our village, and I told one of my male relatives to go and see whether it was a place where I ought to go, and he went for several Sundays, and then said I had better go too. I went constantly after that, and became a church-member. There are now twenty Christians in our village, and they have contributed eight pounds toward the new chapel that is to be built. My children believe as I do, and I have written to my husband that he must worship God. I pray every day that he may live to come back, and that our family may all be Christians.

Chinese women do not know that it is wicked to kill themselves. It is only we who have been taught that we are God's property, that dare not destroy what is His. It is only we that value our lives aright, who know that we have a heaven to go to, and need time to get ready.

CHAPTER XXVIII.

OUT OF THE DEPTHS.

I SUPPOSE that of all the women in this land of China, where there is so much sorrow, there are not many whose lot has been harder than mine. I weep in pity for myself when I think of my past misery, and blush with shame when I consider how great have been my sins. I owe it to my missionary teacher that I now know that my sorrow need not be everlasting, and that my sins may be blotted out. Ever since I learned that there is a heaven and a Redeemer, this world has been a new one for me. My mother was reckoned an unfortunate woman in that she continually bore daughters. She had more than ten of them, though she reared but two. She had but one son. My sister was married when I was born, and my mother decided to keep me alive. My brother was strong, and was the treasure and hope of his parents. They were at that time in comfortable circumstances, owning a good house and several rice-fields. When my brother was twenty-one years old, he was shot in a clan feud, and my earliest recollection is of the distress his death occasioned in our family. I was three years old, and my mother loved me devotedly; but in this country it is of no use to care for girls. They can only be kept till they are fifteen, or thereabouts, and then they must belong wholly to some one else. In some places those who have an only daughter and no sons, can adopt a son and give him their daughter for a wife, but there was no such custom in our village, and so my parents could not do this. That they might not be alone in their old age, and that they might have offerings made at their graves after death, they adopted a son; but he gambled, lost money, stole all the valuables in the house, and ran away. Then they thought that one who had a wife would be more reliable, and hearing of such an one who was parentless, they brought the couple to our home and would have made them their heirs. But there was soon a famine in the land. On our three acres of rice-field, there was not a plant of rice that year. Two crops failed, and food was four times the usual price. My father mortgaged his house and land to get money to keep us from starving. Then word came that the village in which my sister lived was to be burned by the government officials, on account of some criminal who lived there, and my sister soon after brought her clothing and jewellery to my mother for safe keeping. The next day we heard that our village was also to be fired, and my mother took my sister's valuables with our own and deposited them all with an aunt in another village. Just then my adopted brother's wife went away to visit a relative of hers at some distance, and three days later her husband went to our aunt, told her that the affair which endangered our village had been settled, and that my mother had sent him to get all the things in her care. She gave them to him, and he took them to a pawn-shop, got the money for them, hired a sedan-chair for rapid travelling, joined his wife somewhere, and we never heard of either of them again. I was then nine years old. After that the seasons were better, but my father was old and could not work hard, and had to sell his house to pay his debts. He built a very small house, in which we lived.

As my mother loved me much, she had difficulty in finding a husband that she thought good enough for me, and I was not betrothed until I was fifteen, nor married till I was seventeen. My mother would have kept me still longer, only my mother-in-law would not consent. My mother got five pounds in money and a hundred pounds of pastry at my marriage, and she gave me thirty garments, a wash-tub, two lanterns, two clothes-bags, a pillow, a coverlet, and a set of head-ornaments. My mother-in-law lived two miles from my mother's house. She was not unkind to me. When I was twenty-one, my husband went out of the house one morning in good health, and was brought back dead,—shot in a clan feud. Seven months later my oldest son was born. When he was three years old the ancestral property was divided, and my son had his father's share. But there was no one to work the land, and my mother-in-law wanted more sons, and so adopted one in her last son's place. I did not know until he came to the house, that I had a new husband. I was very angry, because I had not been consulted, and because proper precaution had not been taken in ascertaining whether he was a good man. He lived with us only one month. During that time he gambled, lost money, borrowed more on the pretext of going into business, and then ran away. That same year my second son was born. I thought then that I was miserable, but if my trouble had never grown greater I ought to have counted myself a happy woman. My mother-in-law soon told me that the times were hard, and I was young, and she would marry me out of the family. To this she was instigated by my elder sister-in-

L

law, who was selfish and wicked, and seemed born to do me harm. I told her I would support myself by weaving, and that I was willing to starve rather than marry again, and asked her if I had failed in my duty to her, that she meant thus to disgrace me. She said she found no fault in me, but that it was better for me to marry. Soon after, a go-between, a distant relative of mine, came and told me that an honest and kind man wanted me, and persuaded me that I could do nothing wiser than to marry him. I consented, and my mother-in-law got five pounds in money and a hundred pounds of pastry for me, and I had no outfit. She kept my oldest boy, who was her own grandson, and gave me my second son, whom she did not want.

This husband was a farmer, had no parents, and had had no wife before. He had one rice-field which he worked, and I spun and wove to help him to support the family. I had two more sons and one daughter, but we did not keep the latter. It was very hard living, even when my husband was well and could work, but he was taken sick, and though I worked hard I could not fill five mouths and buy medicines. He had consumption for three years, and then we were forced to consider whether we would sell our one rice-field, or one of the children. Without the rice-field those left could not live, and we decided to sell our youngest boy, then three years old, and for him we got five pounds. One month later my husband died. I could not afford the expense of a funeral, with procession, mourning garments, music and a feast, but I bought a coffin for eight shillings, and paid four shillings for the burial. Then with the rice-field, and by my weaving, I managed to support my two remaining boys and myself.

One day I asked my cousin where my uncle was, and heard that he had gone to see Linden Chapel, which was just finished. It could be seen from our village, but I had never been there. I sat and waited till my uncle came past my door, and then accosted him, and asked him if it was a good doctrine that was preached at Linden Chapel, and if it was for women as well as men. He answered that the doctrine was good tidings for all people, and that in seven days more there would be another Sunday, when I could go and hear for myself. The next Sunday I went with my friend, Pearl's mother. A Bible-woman taught us three sentences of a prayer, and we both made up our minds that day to put away the idols from our houses. After hearing the preaching a few more Sundays, we put the idols out, she and I the same day.

Soon after that, my husband's elder brother who had been abroad some years, sent me five pounds by a cousin, the son of the uncle who had directed me to the chapel. My brother-in-law had heard of my husband's death, and knew there was no one but me and my sons to keep up the worship of the ancestors. When the cousin arrived and found that I had become a Christian, he would not give me the money. He beat my uncle, his own father, for going to the chapel, and no one dared take part against him, because he was strong and violent, and we Christians were so disliked. No one would dare beat his father for anything else than being a Christian; and this is the sole occasion on which he could do so and be upheld by his neighbours. I had much controversy with my cousin about the money, and he told me that if I would stop worshipping God, and would worship the family idols, he would give me this money, and that my brother-in-law would send me much more. I told him that I could not well afford to lose the money, but that I could still less afford to lose my soul, and that I should always worship God. The neighbours finally declared that the money ought to be given to me in accordance with the direction in a letter sent with it, and at last my cousin delivered it over. But he wrote to my brother-in-law that I had become a Christian, and so no more money was sent to me. My sons agree with me that whatever we lose on earth we will gain in heaven.

CHAPTER XXIX.

THE MISTS OF MORNING.

WHEN I was very young, I experienced neither joy nor sorrow. My mind was unenlightened and my heart inert, and I reasoned no more than did the cows I tended in my father's fields. My home was in a hamlet, and I was the youngest of a family of four sons and two daughters. My father made salt from sea-water, and my brothers tilled our land. I used to tend the cows, leading them about by a rope fastened to an iron ring in the nose. I often went with my father to the salt-pans, helping him to carry the light tools, and with my brothers to the rice-fields, doing such work as a child might. I also learned to spin, weave, and sew. My brothers taught me some words, but as soon as I began to really know how to read, they said it was not well for women to be learned, and so ceased to teach me. When I was thirteen, my feet were bound, and I could no longer go out in the pleasant fields, nor do any active work. At sixteen I was married into a village near ours. The family into which I went had at that time land and houses, but my husband and his brothers gambled and lost much money, and after I had been there one year they all went away to foreign parts, where they afterward died. My mother-in-law adopted a son and daughter for me, and I lived with her till I was thirty-three years old. By that time we were so reduced in poverty, that I married off my adopted daughter, gave away my adopted son, and married my present husband, who was a widower with a son and two daughters. The son is now abroad, and the daughters are married. My husband is a very upright man, and of so peaceful a disposition that he would sooner be deprived of his rights than quarrel in maintaining them. He was an only son, and his parents were dead, so that we lived by ourselves. He tilled his own land, and some of the ancestral estate, whereby we lived comfortably. Soon after I was married I had a daughter, and named her Light Follower. I did not then know anything of the True Light which she and I were afterward to hear and to follow. Six years later I had another daughter, and named her Jewelled Branch.

We lived three miles from the district city, and one day when my husband was there on business, a cousin of his told him about a chapel that had lately been opened there, and asked him to go and see it. He went, and heard the doctrine from the preacher there, and when he came home he told me all he had heard. I at once said, "That is good doctrine, and I believe it." Then he said, "If you accept this doctrine, you will not burn incense any more, nor go to the temples, nor worship other gods than this Great One;" and I answered, "Very well: I will not," and from that time I never worshipped idols again. My husband went to the chapel on Sundays, and after awhile I went with him. Chinese women do not say "my husband." If they wish to speak affectionately, they say "the children's father;" otherwise they simply say "he." Neither do husbands and wives walk together in the street, nor allow themselves to be seen in each other's company. But after we became Christians, my husband and I went together to the chapel, for we knew that in the beginning God made a man and his wife to be company for each other, and that it was His will to have us unashamed of each other. One day my husband told me that he was coming here to be baptized, and I said I would come too, for if he was going to heaven, I did not wish to be left behind ; so we both came and were baptized the same day. After this my husband's relatives would not let him till the rice-fields with them, because he did not worship the ancestors from whom the fields were inherited, and he gave up his share in the common property. His relatives said that our new God would not help us, and that they would see us starve; but we trusted in the Lord, and did not worship the ancestors. As the little field my husband owned was not enough to support us, and as his brethren were so unfriendly that he could not get work, he had to borrow money to buy food, and was beaten by his creditor when he could not pay. At last we seemed to have no recourse but to sell our daughter Light Follower, then seven years old. She was very fair and gentle, and I had never in her life had occasion to reprove her. We sold her for five pounds to a lady in the district city. This lady was the wife of a government officer, and had only one child, a boy five years old. She bought Light Follower as a slave, and intended to bring her up and sell her as an inferior wife to some rich man. When the master of the house was at home, she was very kind to Light Follower, and gave her enough to eat ; but as soon as he went away, she was very cruel to the child. She made her carry the boy around on her back, and if she fell down, she whipped her. She starved her till she would gladly have picked out and eaten the bitter skins of fruit that had been cast into the gutter, but she was not allowed to do that, lest the neighbours should see her doing it, and thus know how hungry she was. When this woman was in very bad temper, she would heat the tongs, and pinch Light Follower with them, in places where the burn would not be discovered. Light Follower had been there a year and five months when I heard of her misery, and heard that her mistress hated her so that she wished to sell her. I then came and told the Church my trouble, and the members gave me thirty-three shillings. I borrowed twelve and sixpence from each of our two married daughters, and I had three shillings of my own, and the pastor gave me the rest needed to make up the five pounds, and I bought Light Follower back again. But for a long time we were distrusted and blamed by the Church for having sold our daughter.

Six years ago I had a dream, in which I saw a new house, with snowy white walls rising up, as yet unfinished, and it was ours. I told my husband about it, and laughed at myself for dreaming about a new house when we were so poor. But my husband reprimanded me for having so little faith, and said that we would have plenty of benches in our new house, and invite the neighbours to come in and worship God with us in the evenings. We have now the new house, and a garden, and even the benches; but as yet we are the only Christians in our village, and no one comes to worship with us in the evenings. Our son, who is abroad, last year sent home two pounds ten shillings toward rebuilding the house, and we have had new furniture made for it; but it is not yet painted.

Light Follower is a Church-member, and is very obedient and faithful. I shall never bind the feet of my daughters, nor marry them to other than Christians.

CHAPTER XXX.

LIGHT AT EVENTIDE.

I HAVE always lived in the city of Kui Su. My parents were very poor. They had no sons, and I was the second of their three daughters. We were all employed in the making of mock money, used in the worship of gods and spirits. The paper is cut in sheets a few inches square, and a blotch of gilding is put on with a brush in the middle of one side of the sheet. The gilded sheets sell for from a halfpenny to fivepence per hundred, according to their size. They are used on all occasions for idol-worship, in quantities depending on the wealth and the devotion of the worshipper. They are cast burning on the water from the prow of a junk when it starts on a voyage; they are scattered along the road by which a coffin is carried; they are laid, with a stone on one corner, to flutter over graves; they are put on the ground where an excavation is to be made; they are burned before every deity to whom a petition is addressed. Whatever else may be absent from the offerings brought to idols, this paper must not be wanting. It is supposed to be the currency of the spirit-world, and all spirits look kindly on a present of pocket-money.

Even when I was a child, I could earn something in the gilding of this paper, and often worked at it all day and late into the night. If very industrious, I could earn as much as twopence-halfpenny a day.

When I was eleven years old, I was betrothed. My mother then got six pounds for me, and was to have as much more at my marriage; but soon after my betrothal my husband's father died, and his mother was left with three young sons and little property. So it was arranged between her and my parents that she should pay but two pounds more for me, and that I should have no money expended on my wedding outfit. I therefore had nothing new at my marriage but one or two plain tunics.

I was eighteen when I was married, and my husband was twenty-four. There was only one room in my mother-in-law's house, and I had a bed in one corner, and she a bed in another corner. The youngest boy slept with her, and the next to the youngest lived away from home. My mother-in-law was a very severe person. She often complained that the room was too small for four persons to live in, and sought opportunities to make me feel that I was in the way; but I never opened my mouth to reply to her at such times. While she spun, I gilded paper, and drew myself into the smallest possible space, and worked as fast as I could, and cried quietly. When, after four months, I went to visit my own mother, my mother-in-law took my head-dress and all the girlish ornaments I had possessed; and, after I came back, I could never find them again. Two years after I was married, I had a daughter. I was always hungry, and sat at my work even when I was in great pain, not daring to stop, lest I should be more hungry. My mother-in-law scolded me more than ever, saying that there were too many mouths in the family. I had another daughter, but did not keep her. Then I had a son, and all my acquaintances were glad; but my mother-in-law was unkinder than ever. She took no care of me nor of the child; and she left the door open as she went out and came in, so that I constantly shivered with cold. The same day that my son was born, I got up from bed and washed clothes and cooked. I stood on the cold stones at work, and soon had a fever, and was in great pain. The child had not enough to eat, and I secretly told my husband that he must get some glutinous rice with which to feed the baby. He got some and brought it to me, hiding it under his jacket as he came; but my mother-in-law saw it, and reviled him for loving this child more than he loved his mother. The child had fits, and died when eleven days old. I cried over him till my eyelids were swollen so that I could not open them. I cried, but there was no one to pity me. Though unable to open my eyes, I still worked blindly at my paper-gilding, and was scolded if I ate a bowl of porridge. Once, when very hungry, I took an unusual quantity of porridge from the pot, and filled up the deficiency with water; but my mother-in-law discovered what I had done, and reviled me more than ever before. Twice I laid plans for killing myself, but when the time came, I dared not carry out my design.

My husband had learned the trade of a silversmith, and worked in a town twenty miles away, so he was seldom at home. My mother-in-law died when I was thirty-four. Soon after that, my son Kim Kek was born, and I was less unhappy, though we were still very poor. Kim Kek was a thoughtful child; and when he was hungry he would not cry, because he saw it vexed me and hindered my work. I decided to become an ascetic, and to live the life of a Buddhist. People do this when they do not know the True Doctrine, and suppose that by following certain practices they may in some world become insensible to sorrow. For ten years I ate no animal food, wore no earrings, used no hair-oil, had no red colour in my shoes, and worshipped the gods continually. In adopting this course, my husband neither opposed nor commended me. He saw that I had made up my mind to lead a religious life, and acquiesced in it.

About seven years ago, I heard that a chapel had been opened in our city, and after awhile I asked a nephew of mine to take me there, as I knew that he himself sometimes went. But he would not take me, because he was afraid that some of the powerful people in our clan might find it out, and hold him responsible if I should become a Christian. He told the preacher, however, that I wished to hear the gospel, and the preacher came to my house and told me about the true God. My son Kim Kek heard also, and began to go to the chapel on Sundays. Chinese New Year approached, and the time for special worship of the household gods drew near. I was at a loss to know what to do. I was afraid to neglect the family idols, lest they should do me some harm ; and I was afraid to worship them, lest the true God should be displeased with me. After being long tossed to and fro between the old customs and the new truth, a happy idea came to me. I sent for the preacher to come and take the gods away at once and destroy them, so that they need not be worshipped at New Year. Three of them were very large and finely gilded, and sat on a shelf opposite the door, so that one would see them as soon as one entered. As the preacher was taking them down, I bethought myself that my husband would come home, and when he found the gods gone would beat me; and I knew I was too feeble to bear much beating. So I asked the preacher to leave the gods in a corner of the room till I could persuade my husband of their impotence. When my husband came and saw that the gods were displaced, he was angry, but did not beat me. I told him that, if the gods were really able, they would punish me who removed them, and that I alone would have to bear the consequences of their displeasure. He said that, if I and Kim Kek did not want the gods, he would give them to our married daughter. I tried to tell him about the great God whom we all ought to worship, but he said that as soon as he could afford the expense he would have these gods set up again. After he went away again, I had the idols destroyed. The next time he came home, I was out of the house. When he saw that the gods were gone, he jumped up and down and screamed with rage. Kim Kek ran and found me, and we both hid and prayed till my husband was gone out of the house. Then I told Kim Kek that when his father came home at nightfall, he must have warm water and the tub ready for him to bathe, and must be very attentive to his wants, and hand to him everything he wanted to use before he had time to ask for it. We had supper ready, and I sat on the bed sewing and said nothing when he came in, while Kim Kek waited on him. I expected that he would beat and perhaps kill me, and I kept praying to God to soften his heart. He ate his supper and went to bed, and never said a word more about the gods.

I wished to break my Buddhistic vow, but did not know how to do it. Kim Kek told me to boil two eggs, and take them to the chapel and eat them. I hid the eggs under my tunic, and went and told the preacher what I wished to do; and he prayed for me, and I ate the eggs. Thus I made of no avail all the Buddhistic merit that I had accumulated during ten years.

I went to the meetings at the chapel on Sundays, and some of the sisters told me that I was doing wrong in making mock money. They said that a Christian must not follow that occupation. I was much perplexed, for I had no other means of earning my living, and must starve if I did not work. I laid the case before the preacher, and he told me that I should go on gilding paper, and meanwhile constantly pray to God to open for me some other way of earning my food. I did so, and after awhile I came here to learn to read the Bible. I learned to read, and have since been to many distant places to teach the gospel. My husband lives with our married daughter. He is a believer when he is with Christians, and a disbeliever when he is with pagans. I keep praying the Lord to make him a true disciple.

I thank the Lord for making me so happy. During all my youth, my heart was hopeless and my mind was benighted ; but now, when I am old, the Lord has shined upon me, and my path is bright.

CHAPTER XXXI.

HOW A FAMILIAR SPIRIT WAS EJECTED FROM A HOUSEHOLD.—THE STORY TOLD BY TOLERANCE.

THE first thing that I remember in my life is the distress of extreme poverty. My father was a simple-minded man, and in this country such people seldom earn enough to keep their families from starving. He worked in the fields, but his wages were far too small to fill the eight mouths in his house. My mother spun and wove, but we children were all small and hungry, and she had often no resource but to go out begging. I was the eldest of the children, and had four brothers. There had been one other girl born into the family, but my parents were too poor to keep more than one daughter. My father's mother also lived with us, having no son beside my father.

When I was ten years old, my parents pawned me to a rich widow, living eleven miles from our house. She had three little children, and took me as a servant, feeding and clothing me, and giving my parents two pounds ten shillings for me. They could have me back when they repaid the money. I swept and washed and went on errands, and took care of the children. I slept on the brick floor, with no mosquito-bar nor coverlet; but I had sufficient food, and was not overworked. People do not generally oppress young children. I often cried all

The Story told by Tolerance.

night, however, because I was homesick. My grandmother and my mother also cried because I was away from them; and after five months they sold all the pigs we had, and took the money, and came and redeemed me. I was so glad to get home that I did not afterward much mind the pains of poverty.

When I was fifteen, my mother was attacked by a demon, and she could not drive it away. Christians have only to resist the devil, and he flees from them; but people who know nothing about God have only their own strength with which to meet demons, and they have to succumb to them. My mother had violent palpitation of the heart, spasmodic contraction of the muscles, and foaming at the mouth. Then she would speak whatever the demon told her to say, and would do whatever he impelled. My father told her that it was very bad to be a spirit-medium; but, if she was going to be one, she must be an honest one, and never give other than good advice, nor take more than fair pay for her services. She never took more than a penny or three-halfpence from any one who came to her for a consultation with her demon. There were several spirit-mediums in our village, but none who were so popular as my mother became. She has three times walked over beds of burning coals, five or six times washed herself in boiling oil, and once climbed a ladder of knives seventy feet high. There was a dark hole in the river near our village, where two boys and a man had at different times been drawn in and drowned, and it was supposed that an evil spirit lived down there and devoured human beings. My mother, in one of her frenzies, plunged into the hole, dived down out of sight, and brought up a soft white animal, with four legs, and a head like a cat's. It was put under an inverted rice-box, and for a long time nobody dared lift the cover off the captive. When the cover was lifted, the creature was gone. I suppose it had been metamorphosed into something else. The report of my mother's having dragged the evil spirit from its den spread far and wide, and brought many to her for advice.

When I was eighteen, I was married. My husband was a gambler, and his family was so poor that I soon returned to my mother's house, where I have lived ever since. My husband went abroad, and I have not heard from him for many years. I have no children except Cake, a little girl that a cousin gave to me.

When I was twenty-two, my father died, and shortly after, the two young women that my mother had taken as wives for two of my brothers, both died within twenty days. My brothers then said that the familiar spirit was a harmful one, and that they would no longer live in the house with it. The two elder boys went away and became the sons of a wealthy kinsman, the third set up housekeeping apart from us, and the youngest hired himself out to a petty official. My mother was greatly distressed by all this, and thought she would try to rid herself of her possessor; but the demon told her that, if she tried to evict him, she would be the worse for it, and she then dared do nothing for her own salvation.

After awhile, my mother brought two old women, one paralyzed, the other blind, and kept them in her house at her own charges. She did this in order to make merit. It is said that, when one's accounts are balanced on one's entrance into the next world, one good act will set off ten bad ones. My mother hoped, by caring for these helpless women, to cancel some of her demerits. The old women could not even feed themselves, and they made a deal of work for me.

The Story told by Tolerance. 163

Three years ago, a friend of mine came from Kui Su, twenty-four miles away, to visit me. She told me that she had heard from some Bible-women at Kui Su a new doctrine that was very strange and interesting. She expounded it to me, and it seemed to me that what she said was true. I had before heard that there were missionaries at Swatow, who taught people not to worship idols, and I had considered such teaching very reprehensible. My eldest brother, Po Heng, happened to come home while my friend was with me, and he also heard what she said. I told him that, as his feet were strong and large, while mine were bound and weak, he must go to Kui Su for me, and find out all he could about this true God, and then come back and tell me. He went and found the chapel, and stayed there several days with the preacher, Hong An. Hong An taught him, but did not know whether he was a sincere inquirer, or whether he had some sinister object in coming so far and staying at the chapel. He told Po Heng when the next communion gathering would be at Swatow, and that he would do well to go then and meet the assembled brethren. Po Heng came home and told me what he had learned, and the next month he and I came. I got my mother-in-law to come with me, so that she might have her prejudices removed, and not thwart me if in the future I should wish to become a Christian. I went home after a few days, convinced that the doctrines of Jesus were true. I taught my mother, and she gradually believed. As the Holy Spirit came in, the demon went out. When she knew about the true God and trusted in Jesus, she no longer feared the demon; and when he came and agitated her heart and twisted her muscles, she prayed to God till the demon left her. The idols were all put out of the house, and the other members of the family began to believe. The old blind woman believed as soon as she heard. She still lives with us, and worships God. The paralytic would not listen to the gospel, and declared that the idols should not be put out of the house. She was a great trial to us when we found that she would not acquiesce in our being Christians; but in only a month or two after she began to oppose us, she died.

All the neighbours protested against my mother's ceasing to interpret the will of the gods to them. When they saw that Po Heng and I were determined to be Christians, they urged my mother to separate herself from us, and continue her old occupation. But we held to our mother, and finally brought her, heart and all, with us. We have less money than we had when my mother was a spirit-medium; but we have what is worth more than money, a knowledge of the truth, and the joy that comes from the consciousness that we are in the way to heaven.

When Po Heng began to believe, his adopted mother, who is quite wealthy, and who gave to him, as to her own sons, a monthly allowance of rice, told him that if he became a Christian he would have no more rice from her bins. When he was baptized, she did cut off his allowance; but now she sees that he is a better son than ever before, and she again gives him his stipend. Though he has now become a preacher, she loves him more than ever, and is very proud of him.

Po Heng's wife was very ill last year; and once, when Po Heng and I returned home from the communion at Swatow, we found her at the point of death. The neighbours told Po Heng to hasten and call the best physicians;

The Story told by Tolerance.

but I told him we must not put our rust in physicians, but in God: we were all Christians, and, if we knelt around her bed and prayed to God, He would cure her. The whole family was called together, even the little children; and all joined in prayer for the immediate recovery of the invalid. The next morning she was much better, and in a few days she got well.

Then we wanted to get a wife for Po U, my youngest brother. Wives were very dear, and cost at least twenty pounds. The heathen people around us did not want their daughters to marry into a Christian family, and we did not want to have any one in our family who would not be a Christian. There was no Christian near us who had a daughter of a suitable age for Po U, and the distant Christians would not let their daughters go far from home to marry. We were much troubled by the difficulties of the case. Just then we heard of a young woman who might be had for a small sum. She had been a very bright, handsome girl, and had been married to a man who was an idiot. She had cried night and day after she was taken to her husband's house, and had become insane through grief. Her husband's parents were afraid she would kill herself or them, and wanted to be rid of her. We talked the matter over in our family, and decided that, as her derangement of mind had been caused by misery, she would, when restored to reason, embrace the religion of those who should make her happy. We knew that Jesus healed the sick and cast out demons; and we thought we might take this girl, trusting Him to cure her in answer to our prayers. We therefore bought her, and brought her home as a wife for Po U. Po U had consented willingly in our plans, but when he saw how crazy his wife was, his faith failed, and he ran away to foreign parts. The rest of us prayed for her constantly, and in a few months she was perfectly well.

The familiar spirit troubles my mother no more. Every member of our household is a believer, and several of our neighbours come to our house for Sunday worship. But there are three thousand people in our clan, and only twelve of them are Christians. Besides there are more villages than I can count around the one in which my mother-in-law lives; and no one preaches the gospel in any of them.

CHAPTER XXXII.

THE PILLARS OF THE CHURCH AT SOUTH SPUR.

SOUTH SPUR is a hamlet of a few hundreds of people. A few years ago there was no church there, and no one there had heard of Jehovah. The nearest chapel was at Cannon Stand, twelve miles away. A woman named Lily, long resident at South Spur, quarrelled with her husband, and he beat her and reviled her mother. Such accidents happen even in the best Chinese families. To the beating she was not unaccustomed, and that she could bear; but the reviling of her mother was something which no woman of spirit would permit, and which public opinion would not justify. She shut herself up in her room, the walls of which were dotted with little shelves holding idols of which she was a devout worshipper. Some of these gods she had experimentally found to be of no use, and had cast them out of her confidence. Before the others she every day placed fresh cups of tea, kneeling while she fanned the fire to boil the water for this sacred tea, and then offering it with prostrations and incense. After quarrelling with her husband on this occasion, she sat herself down in her trouble before her gods; but they only looked down upon her dumbly. She sought an interpreter, a sorceress who could tell her the mind of her idols, and through this sorceress she learned, that in the opinion of the gods, she ought to leave her family and go into a Buddhist nunnery for the rest of her life. So she gave direction to a faithful servant concerning the care of her two little boys, and wrote a paper to tell them where they would find their mother when they should be grown up. Then she hired an old woman, who knew the way, to guide her in her flight to a nunnery near the Departmental City. She made her escape unseen from her own village, and under the guidance of the old dame walked to Cannon Stand, where they were to take a boat to the city. At Cannon Stand they found they must wait for some hours for the turn of the tide, and they did not know what to do in the interval. The old dame said, "I have been told there is a chapel here at Cannon Stand, and that there are good women in it, who teach a new doctrine. I do not know what sort of a thing a chapel is, nor what is the doctrine which is taught, but we have nothing else to do, and might go and see what it is like." So the two made inquiry here and there till they found the chapel, where Keepsake greeted them, and' finding them unwilling to converse, asked them to sit down and hear a story. So they sat down and heard that God made the world, and created man; that man sinned against God and put idols in His place; that the Son of God so loved the world that He came to the earth to bring spiritual light and truth to man, and to save from sin all who should believe and follow Him. This story so wrought on the mind of the fugitive that she told the narrator her own history, and asked what she should do in order to obey God. Keepsake advised her to relinquish her purpose of going to the nunnery, and to stay at the chapel a few days and hear more of these truths. She stayed four days, while the old dame went back to South Spur and told the alarmed and penitent husband where his wife was. Then the old dame came again for her, and she went home with juster ideas of duty. After awhile she returned for further instruction, and then Keepsake and other teachers went to her house and taught her and her neighbours. At that time she told me her story as follows :—

LILY'S STORY.

"From the earliest age I was very fond of going about everywhere worshipping the gods. I was the youngest in our family, and because I was so, was always anxious lest those who loved me should not live as long as I. My grandfather was a squire, and my father was called the young squire. When I was seventeen years old I was married to the son of a squire. In my own home I was accustomed to be waited upon. My brother's wife attended upon me, and usually when I awoke in the morning I found my breakfast ready and waiting beside my bed. I had nothing to do, and no care, and was as plump and round as a quail. But after I was married I had to wait upon my husband's parents, as well as upon his grandmother who lived with them ; and I had to offer them their tea and everything else kneeling, as is the custom in rich and powerful families. I had also to take care of the pigs and fowls, and to carry water and do the washing ; and as I was the fifth and youngest son's wife, all the heaviest work came upon me. Before I was married my finger-nails were four inches long, as is the fashion among those who need not work. These I had to cut off, that they should not embarrass me in the drudgery I had to perform in my husband's house. I had to turn the mill for hulling rice. Of my three sisters-in-law, two were strong, and had to help to hull the rice; but the other one was weakly, and she did the cooking. The fourth son had died without a wife. My two sisters-in-law set me to turn the mill, while they sifted the rice, so I devised a plan by which they should have to help me at the mill. I asked one of them to let me change work with her awhile, knowing I was awkward at sifting and thinking I would sift very slowly, so that the other sifter, who was expert, would have the bulk of the work to do. But my plan did not succeed, for the other sifter divided the rice into two equal portions, and told me that when she had sifted her portion she would take a rest until I finished mine. So I found the sifting as hard as turning the mill. I first stayed in my husband's house four months, and then I went to my old home, very thin and sad, and stayed eight months with my own mother. I said nothing about my troubles, and was as happy as the day was long; but when the eight months came to an end, and I had to go back to my father-in-law's, I wept and wailed aloud, and all my clothes had to be put on me by main force, and when they began to paint my face, I fought and howled, and would not be made ready. I then told my father how hard I had to work, and declared I would not go back. Then he said he had made a great mistake in marrying his daughter to farming people who were so saving, and that he would go and rate them for wearing his plump daughter down to a shadow in four months. I knew if he did this they would become aware that I had complained of them, and they would therefore make my life harder than ever. So I besought him not to say a word to them, and said I would at once go back quietly and do my duty. Then my father said he would buy a servant for me; but as there was none to be

The Pillars of the Church at South Spur. 171

bought on the instant, he borrowed one from my brother's wife, and I took this borrowed slave with me.

"My mother-in-law used to put many things, such as oil-cakes and sugar, in my room in my care, and others in the household had to come to me to get these things for use. I, being the youngest, did not dare to tell them not to take too much, and they often did so, leaving me with no way of defending myself against the suspicion of having used the things myself. So I and my servant used to cry very often over our hard lot. My mother-in-law was much displeased because my handmaid and I cried together, and because I liked my servant more than I liked my husband; so she sent the girl home after she had been with me only eleven days, pretending that she thought my brother's wife would want her. Then my father bought a slave and sent her to me. She was thirteen years old, and cost only five pounds. We thought this wonderfully cheap, not knowing that she had any disease; but after a few days we learned that she had fits, and she frightened me almost out of my senses when she fell into one; and so, as the money for her had not been paid, she was sent back to her people. My father next bought a six-year-old girl for me, paying three pounds for her, and thinking that I could train her to work. But she was a great care to me, as I had to bathe and dress her, and sew for her; and moreover she was a little thief, and stole charcoal and cakes, and laid hands on whatever she could eat. So I only kept her until she was ten years old, and then sold her for six pounds.

"I had no children until I was twenty-three years old, and the family all mocked at me meanwhile and said I was a 'stone' woman. My own mother was greatly grieved on my account, and went far and near seeking gods who were powerful in giving fruitfulness, making offerings to them in my behalf. I myself became a devotee of Buddha, and fasted often, and had in my room as many as twenty idols which I worshipped daily, and before which I kept lamps burning. Having been told by a witch to do so, I stole a rice-bowl from a woman who was the mother of many sons, and made of it a new god of the bedstead. I had to put into the bottom of the bowl two scraps of red silk, two yeast-cakes, and twelve leaves taken from twelve kinds of thornless plants, and on these pack ashes from the kitchen range, or from a censer. This constitutes the god of the bedstead, which is kept on a shelf under or over the bed, and is worshipped at the new and the full moon by all women, from the time of marriage until the youngest child is fifteen years old. This is the god that is depended upon to give and preserve children. Soon after I had set up a new god of the bedstead I had two children that did not live, and then, when I was twenty-five, my son, Jun Soi, was born. Just before that my own father died; and I, remembering how he had loved me, had a great quantity of paper clothing, and a trunk, and pipes holding real tobacco, made to burn at his funeral with a scroll on which was written a verse of my own composition, saying, 'Remembering my father, I gaze at the clouds and weep bitterly, because those whom death divides meet no more.' On account of my great devotion to the gods, all the people of our village respected me, and my husband yielded to my opinions, and followed my advice even in worldly affairs. Now that I have become a Christian, I have lost the esteem of my neighbours, but I have gained what is of even greater value."

Lily persisted against great obstacles in her Christian career, and has been so happy as to lead her husband to join her. Her own mother, now aged, has also, through her influence, become a Christian, and so have several others among her friends and kindred. Lily is one of the six or seven bound-footed women in the Swatow church who, influenced by Christian principle, have unbound their feet, and after long and painful effort forced the toes back into their natural position, so as to wear shoes like those whose feet have never been bound. Among others taught first by Lily is her neighbour Treasure, a widow with one adopted son. Treasure's account of herself shows well the path by which the mind of a Chinese woman moves waveringly on from polytheism to monotheism.

TREASURE'S STORY.

"I was born of rich parents near Cannon Stand. Those belonging to a more powerful branch of our clan, seized, during a clan feud, the estate of my parents, and they, after spending all they had in an unsuccessful law-suit, moved to the Departmental City. There they married me, when I was sixteen, to a lad a year younger than I. Those who are rich want their sons to marry when very young, so that they may soon have male descendants; and as those younger than my husband would have been too young to marry, they got me, who was a year older, for a wife for him. I had three daughters, and then a son that died when he was ten days old, and then another daughter. I kept the eldest daughter, and she lived till she was nine years old. All the other daughters were put into a hod and thrown alive into the river, one each year. My husband got a chair-bearer to carry them off and drown them. I did not feel sorry when the little girls were carried away, and did not cry. I was vexed because they were not boys, and I did not want them, and I hoped to have sons the sooner if I did not keep the girls. I had not then heard of God, and I did not think that what I did was wrong. When I was twenty-seven years old my husband died, telling me in dying that I must not marry again. In our village it is the custom for those who have no sons to adopt as an heir the child of some relative of the same surname, and such an one must be sought for eight years before one of another surname can be adopted. It may be that a relative has become reduced in circumstances, and then he will sell a son as heir to another. I waited and sought a son for nearly eight years, and then got a second cousin of my husband's. The boy was named Illustrious Ancestry, and was eight years old. His father owed me twelve pounds, and could not pay it. The debt, with the interest and the go-between's fees, came to twenty pounds. After the bargain was made, and before Illustrious Ancestry was brought home, the wife of my husband's younger brother gave birth to a son, and I, holding the common superstition that for four months after the birth of a child evil influences hang about the house, delayed the bringing home of my son. But before the four months had passed, my father-in-law died, and then my son had to be brought home, that he might carry the censer in the obsequies. This is always done by the son of the eldest son. We had five Buddhist priests and their assistants to perform the funeral rites, and we burned more than twenty pounds' worth of paper clothing; but my father-in-law is not yet buried, though he has been dead seven years.

The Pillars of the Church at South Spur.

"Three years ago I heard that a female preacher had come to our village, and was staying at Lily's house. I did not know what sort of a being a 'preacher' might be, as I had never seen one, and I thought perhaps it was a monstrous or a deformed person. Formerly Lily and I had sewn together, and had been great friends, but I had lately been much prejudiced against Lily because people talked so much about her being a Christian, saying she had become a courtesan, and I had not been at her house for a long time. But I wanted to see what a preacher was, and so I went to Lily's door, and Lily greeted me, and introduced me to Keepsake. Keepsake took me by the hand and led me to a seat, and taught me. I thought the doctrine so good that I at once made up my mind that I would go to the chapel at Cannon Stand and hear more of it. Keepsake stayed only one day in our village, but she spoke the gospel all the time she was there, and would talk of nothing else. After she went back to Cannon Stand she sent a letter to Lily, and told her which day was Sunday, and that she must then come to the chapel, and bring me with her. So I made up my mind to go and see for myself how much was true and how much was false of all that was popularly said against the Christians. That night I dreamed that I was daubed all over with filth. In the morning I told my dream to my sister-in-law, and she said my dream was a sign from our dead father-in-law that my good name would be tarnished if I went to the chapel, so I did not go. Some time after I borrowed Lily's Bible and read in it, and my pig immediately died. So I took the Bible back to Lily, not daring to keep it longer in the house, and I was more afraid than ever of the new doctrines. But after awhile my heart desired to hear more of the gospel, and I went and asked Lily to tell me all that she knew about the Great God. Lily taught me to pray, and I began to ask a blessing before eating my meals, and to pray before I went to sleep. I had only begun to do this when sixteen of my hens were stolen. Then I thought the gods were taking vengeance on me for thinking about Jesus, and I prayed no more. Then Tolerance came to our village, and stayed with Lily, and taught women; and I remembered that long before, when I went to consult a spirit-medium in the village where Tolerance lived, Tolerance had asked me to take supper with her, and so I thought it would be only polite for me to invite Tolerance to take supper with me; but I did not mean to listen to any more doctrine. When Tolerance came, she spoke the gospel all the time, even while eating, and it was really so good that I would not let her go, but persuaded her to stay all night, that I might hear more; and I was so pleased with what I heard that I did not sleep a wink all night long. In the morning I said to Illustrious Ancestry, 'My son, I think this is right doctrine, but if we follow it we shall be despised.' He answered, saying, 'Mother, if it be right doctrine, let us follow it, and endure being despised.' And so we became Christians."

After this decision, mother and son, being twelve miles from a chapel, kept the Sabbath at home. One Sunday Treasure's brother-in-law came in, and said, "We have had enough of this. You no longer worship the ancestors, nor give heed to the family idols. Say now whether you will relinquish this new religion, and remain in your home, or adhere to your new faith, and be driven out of this house and this village." Treasure answered, "Having learned that there is a True God, I must

The Pillars of the Church at South Spur.

worship Him. Do with me as you may, I must follow Christ, for there is a crown of life for those who, being persecuted for His sake, are faithful unto death." Her brother-in-law took off his wooden shoe, and beat Treasure on her bound feet as she knelt, until she was unable to stand. He then dragged her into the street, and told two chair-bearers to carry her so far away that she could never come back. At her direction they carried her to the chapel at Cannon Stand, where the Christian women cared for her until she was brought to the Training School at Swatow. Her brother-in-law eventually allowed her to return home. She has done much work as an evangelist in her own and neighbouring hamlets; her brother has become a Christian, and the brother-in-law who beat her goes sometimes to hear the preacher. A chapel has been erected at South Spur, toward the building of which Lily and her husband gave seven pounds, while Treasure gave five. And this is a list of the furniture in Treasure's house. The house is eight feet wide and sixteen feet deep. The walls are of sun-dried blocks of mud, and there is no floor. A bedstead in the farther end of the room has above it a row of pine shelves, on which clothing is laid. The space underneath the bedstead is used as a store-room. The furniture consists of two pine tables, two feet by three; two pine cupboards, one yard square and one foot deep; a large splint basket for holding unhulled rice, and seven small baskets; two flat baskets used for drying rice in the sun; one washtub; two press-boards; two trestles; one high stool on which she sits when she sews, and one low stool on which she sits at the washtub; one counting-board; two sieves; a mason-work range for cooking; one paper lantern, and some dishes. On the top of the bedstead was stored a rude spinning-wheel; from the roof-beams were suspended three hooks, forked branches of trees, used to hang baskets upon. A loom owned in shares by several women was in the room, and on this Treasure was weaving a piece of cloth, getting fifteen-pence for weaving twenty yards.

CHAPTER XXXIII.

SILVER FLOWER'S ACCOUNT OF HERSELF.

I WAS born at the village of Kam E, thirty-five miles west from here. It was a village of about a thousand people; on a plain, but with many mountains in sight. In the level land were the fertile rice fields; in rougher places were the sugar-cane and sweet potato gardens. The mountains were bare and sterile, and used only as burying grounds. There were many other villages in sight from ours, and the people in nearly all of them were of the surname Go or Kang. In our village there were people of both the Go and the Kang families. My father belonged to the Go clan. He was one of the rich men in our village. We had a large and handsome house. There was a main room twenty feet square, with red tiles for the floor, and the rafters painted red and blue, and pictures painted on the plastered walls; and there were several sleeping rooms, a kitchen, a court open to the sky, and a well. I was the eldest child, and my parents loved me, and named me Silver Flower.

But when I was three years old, all belonging to the Go clan had to flee from the village of Kam E. In another village two women, one of the clan Go and one of the clan Kang, had hard words with each other, and from words came to blows. Then some other women, and finally the men of the two families, entered into the fray; and at last the whole of the two clans, Go and Kang, were at war with each other. There were some twenty villages on each side involved in the feud, and the fighting was continual. As the Kangs were stronger than the Gos in the village of Kam E, my father had to move out. He sold his house very cheaply, and quickly and secretly removed his furniture to a village where all were of the Go clan. There he rented a small house, and we lived very poorly. A great many people had been killed in the feud; the fields had not been properly cultivated, and there was a famine in the land. Rice was four shillings a peck, more than twice its usual cost. My father spent all he had got for his house, and as he could not get enough from his lands to feed his family, he gradually sold his fields, till we had nothing but what he earned as a day labourer; and as mouths multiplied in the house, it was difficult to fill them.

My parents were always kind to me, and would gladly have kept me at home till I was older, but my father died, and when I was fourteen my mother was forced to marry me. I went into a family in another village, and she got two pounds for me. I had never seen any of that family before I went to live in it. My husband, who was just my own age, hated me as soon as he saw me. There are a great many couples who hate at first sight. My mother-in-law was not unkind to me. I cooked the rice, fed the ducks and pigs, and helped her in the house all I could. But my husband was very cruel to me; he would not let me sleep beside him on the pine boards of the bedstead, but made me lie on the mud floor beside the bed; he had the coverlet, and I had nothing over me, and I used to lie and shiver

Silver Flower's Account of Herself. 181

all night. I did not tell any one how he treated me, lest that should make him more cruel. But he got to hating me so that every night he took a knife to bed with him, and told me that he would keep it there ready to kill me if he felt the desire to do it in the night. My mother-in-law saw how he hated me, and fearing the consequences of keeping me with him, she engaged a match-maker to marry me to some one else, and when I was sixteen I was again married, to a man at the village of Be Chia.

My own mother did not know of this second marriage, neither did I myself, until the pledges binding the bargain were exchanged, and it was too late to demur. My mother-in-law had received five pounds for me. This second husband was twenty-seven years old, and a gambler. His father was dead; the ancestral property had been divided among the sons, and the mother lived with her children, going daily to the house of each by turn. When my husband got me he had some money that he had won in gambling, but he soon lost it all, and then he beat me. He would often be away from home a month at a time, going even to distant places, and following theatres about, to gamble. It was of no use to expostulate with him—a gambler does not reform. I have heard of one who cut off his right hand to prevent his gambling any more, but he went right on gambling with his left hand.

My husband could not stop, and continually lost money. There was nothing for his mother to eat, and she ceased to come to our house for any meals, but lived with her other sons. I had then three children— two boys and a girl. It seemed likely that we should starve. My husband had no money to gamble with, either. He said to me: "You have a hard time with me; the children are thin, and you are miserable; it would be much better for you to be married to some kind man who would give you enough to eat. I will find such an one, and marry you to him. I myself am going away to foreign countries to seek my fortune, and I shall never come back." I assented to this, for I saw that the children would otherwise starve.

So my husband himself secretly took me and the children to Kam E, the village in which I was born, and to the house of the man to whom he had engaged me. He got five pounds for me and the children. He did not let any one know about my going, because if people had known it, all the poor of the village would have come out and intercepted us on the road, and made him pay them a fine before we went on. That is the way people do when a man marries off a wife that has borne him children. I did not cry at all when he left me, for I thought I could be no more wretched than I had been with him. He spent the money he got for me in gambling, and did not go to foreign parts, but died soon afterward. I was then twenty-four years old, my oldest son was five years old, and my daughter ten months old. This third husband was thirty-five years old. He had had no wife before, and his father and mother were both dead. He did not gamble, nor smoke opium, and was good-tempered. He had a little land, and rented a house in which we lived. He worked in the fields, tilling his own land and some that he worked on shares. He was very industrious and economical, but when we had more children it was hard work to feed them all. I had four more sons and five daughters. The boys we knew could by-and-by help their father in the fields; but we thought the girls a greater burden than we could bear, and we destroyed four of them. I was always alone when they were born. Had I had an old neighbour with me at the time, she would have expected a present of at least tenpence done up in red paper, a piece of pork, and an invitation to supper afterward. We could not afford such expense. My husband threw the little girls into the river, after stifling them. I am a great sinner; no less a Saviour than Jesus could save one who has sinned so deeply as I. Now, when I think of these children, my heart is full of anguish. I lie awake at night and wonder that such a sin can really be blotted out; but then I did not know God's commandments, and only thought how unprofitable girls were.

When my fourth son was two years old, I was pounding rice in the house, and the children were playing outside the door. A neighbour came and took my little boy up in her arms, and said she would take care of him while I pounded the rice. She took him to see the new house of the richest man in our village. The house was just finished, and many people went to see it. While she was there the owner of the house came in, and noticed my beautiful boy, and asked whose he was. She told him, and said there was a house full of children in the home he came from. The rich man then said: "If those people have so many, then they may as well let me have this one." The neighbour hastened back and reported what the rich man had said, and I at once replied that no one else wanted my boy so much as I wanted him; but my husband, who had just come in, heard it, and said it would be better both for us and for the boy if he were a rich man's son. The neighbour then went and told the rich man that she thought he could get the boy; and the rich man found out the child's birthday, and had a horoscope cast, to see whether the child would bring good fortune with him or not. Finding the omens favourable, he again sent the neighbour to negotiate for the child. I was never willing to let the boy go, but my husband argued with me, saying it would be an excellent thing for us. The rich man was powerful in the village, and said he would exert his influence in our behalf, in any troubles that might arise for us in the future. He gave us at once a house worth twenty pounds. I cried incessantly for a month after the child was taken away. Then my youngest son, Teng In, was born, and he comforted me somewhat. The son that was sold away is now grown; he knows that I am his mother, but he never speaks to me, fearing that his present mother would be offended if she knew it.

When my eldest daughter was thirteen years old, a match-maker came, and we betrothed her to a young man, taking four pounds as pledge money. Before she was married, however, the young man was shot, and we paid back the pledge money to his parents. The matchmaker gets twelve shillings and sixpence for each match; a third from the bride's parents, and two-thirds from the groom's parents. Afterwards we betrothed my daughter again, and she was married that same year. I also took a wife for my eldest son, and brought her home to live with me.

The years were very often unfavourable for the rice crops, and the times were hard. There were several years in succession when we got almost nothing from the land. My husband spent from two to four pounds a year for fertilizers, and then reaped no crop; we had to eat meanwhile, and finally my husband sold all his land to pay his debts, and yet lacked twenty pounds to meet all. Then my second and third sons said they would go abroad, and see if they could earn money; and they went away to Singapore. The elder died there soon after he went, and from the other I have not heard for years; he ceased to write or send money to me as soon as he heard that I had become a Christian. I betrothed my youngest daughter, and she went away when only seven years old to live with her future mother-in-law.

I was then forty-three years old, and had in my house only my husband, my oldest son and his wife, and my youngest son, Teng In. One day my mother came seven miles to see me, and she told me that a friend of hers, who, like her, was a Buddhist, and ate no animal food, and was trying to make merit for the next world, had a grandson who had become a worshipper of a strange god. She said that at Kit Ie, the District City, a different kind of temple had been established; there was no god in it, and people went there once in seven days. She did not understand what they did, but it was all very queer, and contrary to the common ideas of things. I told her that if she would go with me, we would make a journey to Kit Ie, and see what the new god was; and we fixed a time, and my mother again came, and we went together. It was ten miles, and we walked all the way, and when we got to the city we stopped at a Buddhist hostel, where my mother was acquainted, and they told us where the chapel was, and that it was Sunday. We went to the chapel, and there were many people sitting and listening to Preacher Hu. I did not in the least understand what he was talking about, but I listened till they knelt down to pray, and then I was frightened. I did not see what they were kneeling to, and I ran away into one of the small rooms, and waited till they got up. Mother and I went back to the hostel to stay that night, and were going home the next morning. I woke up about midnight, and began thinking about the chapel. I felt very curious to know why that preacher had been talking so earnestly. I tried to remember what he said, but it was all about something I had never before heard of, and I could not in my own mind get the slightest clue to what it was that he was so emphatic about. After puzzling my head about it half the night, I determined that I would in the morning go again to the chapel, and see if I could find out what it all meant. It was God who made me wake up at midnight that night; if I had not done so, I should never have gone again to the chapel, and should not now be a Christian. In the morning mother and I again went to the chapel, and an old woman and her granddaughter were there, and they asked us to sit down, and told us about the doctrine taught there; but still I did not understand it at all. After it got late, and the time had come when we must go home, we started, and the old woman said to a man who was there, "Brother Kan, as you live out on the road where these women are going, you go along with them, and teach them by the way." So Brother Kan came with us, and as we walked he talked, and before we got home I knew where the true God was, and had made up my mind to worship Him.

I told all I had heard to my husband, and he went to the chapel once with me; but after he got back, the neighbours said so much about it, that he would go

Silver Flower's Account of Herself. 187

no more. I kept on going by myself, however. I used to get dreadfully frightened on the road sometimes, especially when I stayed to the afternoon meeting, and it would be dark before I got home. The road was a lonely one, and people said there were tigers along the loneliest parts. I was not afraid of demons, for I had already learned that God has power over all demons, and will protect His children from them; but I did not know whether He would let tigers bite me. My heart used to beat so hard in the lonesomest places, that I could hardly breathe. I would run very fast, too, and in this way I once left behind and lost my head ornaments, and once my scarf. Once when I had run till I was exhausted, and my heart was beating as if it would burst, I saw a man carrying a big bundle on the road before me. I ceased at once to be afraid, and walked quietly along after him a long way. Suddenly he disappeared, where there was no turn of the road, and no house. I have always thought that this man was an apparition that God sent to calm my terror, when I was ready to die of fear.

I wanted to put all the idols out ot the house, but my husband would not hear of such a thing. I did, however, throw away the god of the bedstead. This is a rice bowl, filled with ashes from the kitchen furnace, packed solid, and stuck full of incense sticks. Every young married woman has this put under her bed, and she and her children worship it at least four times a year, putting it up on the bedstead, setting fish, pork, eggs, rice, and cakes before it, and prostrating themselves to pray for a blessing. This they do till the youngest child is fifteen years old. Then they empty the bowl, and keep it carefully where it will not be broken. This is the god that is depended upon to give and preserve children.

About this time Preacher Hu asked me if I did not think I ought to be baptized; and I came here to Swatow, and was received into the Church. Almost as soon as I got back home I was taken sick. I was sick month after month, and all my acquaintances said it was because I had neglected the idols, and taken away the god of the bedstead. They wearied me with their importunities; there was not a Christian in our village for me to speak with; I was worn out with sickness, and my faith failed. I bought paper money and incense, and again worshipped what God abhors. But I got no better, and I was much troubled in my mind about what I had done. I resolved that whether I lived or died, I would have nothing more to do with idols. I got somewhat better, and went again to the chapel. My daughter-in-law was so angry at me for going, that, as I was starting, she caught hold of one of my fingers, and twisted it out of joint. I took my youngest son, Teng In, with me, and was no more afraid on the road.

Then my husband died, and the house and furniture were divided, and I put all the idols out of the part that belonged to me and Teng In. I was then taken sick again, and Teng In went to the chapel alone. I used to sit out at the end of the road and watch for his coming back, and sometimes I was greatly distressed about him, for in those days people were often kidnapped on the road and held for ransom. I would watch till I could see his little white trousers away off through the gloaming, and then my heart would be full of joy. After a while he told me that the next Sunday, several believers from Kit Ie were coming down to Swatow to be baptized, and he wanted to come with them and see the baptism, for he had never seen one. He came, and was away from home four days. He got back at midnight, and knocked at the door, and before I had opened it he called out, "Mother, I have been baptized!" I was astonished, for I did not think he could have answered the questions the brethren ask the candidates for admission to the Church, and he was only fifteen years old. But I was very glad.

I was not able to go myself to visit my friends; but my mother came to see me, and I reasoned with her till she believed. I also made her go and tell the gospel to my younger sister, who lives six miles off. My sister's husband told her he would kill her if she went to the chapel, and she dared not go until he went away to foreign parts. Then she went; but when he heard of it, he ceased to send any money to support her and her children.

I kept talking to one of my neighbours about Jesus, and at first she was so offended, that sometimes she would not come near me, nor speak to me for days; but little by little she believed, and began to go to the chapel on Sundays with Teng In. She is now the Bible-woman called Fragrant Love. My daughter-in-law also began to believe; and when people came along selling charms against evil spirits, she would not buy them, but would say, "I do not want such things: I trust in none but the great God in heaven to keep us from harm." Now, my mother, my sister, one of my sons, my daughter-in-law, and some of my other relatives are Christians. My little grandson always asks a blessing before he eats his rice. I have been to the family into which my eldest daughter is married, and told them about the true God. At first they were inclined to heed me; but one of the boys, in riding to the fields on a water-buffalo, fell off and was found insensible in the furrow. They would have prayed to God for him, but the neighbours said, "Do not do it. Run quickly and get gilt-paper and incense sticks, and worship the god of the field." They did so, and the boy recovered. Now the whole family are hardened against God.

I did not myself get well until you called me to come here and learn to read three years ago. I studied for four months, and was well enough to go out as a Bible-woman. I have been to almost a hundred different villages. I am now fifty-one. God is good to me, and if I have health, so that I can go on doing His work till the end of my life, I shall be wholly content.

CHAPTER XXXIV.

LANGUAGE, LITERATURE, AND FOLK-LORE.

AMONG all classes in China, learning is highly esteemed and earnestly sought. Schools for boys, supported by voluntary contributions, exist in almost every village, and may be attended even by those who cannot afford to pay for tuition. As a matter of fact, scarcely any women, and but a very small portion of the men, know how to read; but the highest offices below the throne are open to the poorest in the land, as the reward of literary attainment. Stories are told of a poor student who bored a hole through the wall of his house, that he might have the advantage of his neigbour's light; and of a boy who fastened his book to the horns of his ox, that he might learn while ploughing; and of a discouraged scholar, who was impelled to renewed exertion by hearing a woman, who was rubbing a crowbar on a stone, say that she wanted a needle, and having only the crowbar, was determined to rub it down to the required size.

Every attainment in literature offers immediate rewards in social esteem and pecuniary advantages. Examinations are frequently held in the district cities, and those who succeed in them may attend the examinations held twice in three years at the Departmental City, and conducted by the prefect of the department, and chancellors from Peking. Those who creditably pass this examination have conferred upon them the degree of Siu Chai, or Promising Talent. They are thereafter exempt from corporal punishment, are sure of lucrative positions as teachers or scribes, and are held in high honour in their native towns.

Twice in three years an examination is held in the provincial capitals; and all those who have taken the degree of Siu Chai may be examined for the higher degree of Ku Jin, or Promoted Men. Each candidate is shut up alone in a small cell, into which he is allowed to take nothing but writing materials and a little food, and is required to write five essays and poems on given subjects. A mistake in a single letter or quotation causes his name to be erased from the list of competitors. After a three days' examination, some tens out of several hundreds of candidates attain the second degree. These may afterwards appear at the examinations at Peking, and compete for the higher degree of Chin Su, or Advanced Scholar. Those who pass this third examination may be appointed to office, and are sure of eminent situations. All the district magistrates in the fourteen hundred and six districts of the eighteen provinces have received the degree of Chin Su.

Afterward the advanced scholar may, by continued study, and a still severer examination in the emperor's palace, become a member of the Imperial Academy, from which the highest officers of the empire are chosen.

China Proper has one written and seven spoken languages. The written language is not spoken in any part of the Empire, and the spoken languages, except the Mandarin, are not written. If an unlearned mother wished to send a letter to her son in a neigh-

Language, Literature, and Folk-Lore. 193

bouring town, she would go to a scribe, and tell him in the colloquial tongue what she wished to say to her son; the scribe would write the message in the language of books, and would receive a halfpenny or more for his services. The letter would then be committed to a letter-carrier, who would collect from the recipient the amount of postage noted on the cover, and varying with the importance of the contents. The son, if not himself a scholar, would take the letter to a scribe, who would give him in the spoken dialect an oral interpretation of the letter. The message would have been translated into and then out of the written language in going from mother to son.

The origin of the written language antedates any existing history, and its correct pronunciation is unknown. It is a system of hieroglyphics, passionately admired by scholars, and deeply reverenced by the unlearned. Eight centuries before Christ, these symbols were traced on tablets of bamboo with a sharp metal stylus. Each character represents a monosyllabic word, and is made up of one or more of the two hundred and fourteen primitives, radicals, or letters which form the alphabet. There are forty thousand characters in the standard lexicon, but only about six thousand are generally used, and a knowledge of three thousand enables one, with occasional reference to a dictionary, to read many books intelligently. The characters are usually arranged in vertical lines, to be read downward, beginning at the right. The first book given to the scholar is the trimetrical classic, which contains four hundred different words, in rhymed lines of three words. It has been used for six centuries by beginners. Its opening lines are these:—

> Man at birth
> By nature good,
> In instinct similar,
> In practice diverging.

Having mastered this primer, the student may take the one thousand character essay, which is said to have been composed by a man who was supplied when in prison with this number of different words, and to have been required to make them into a poem. He performed his task in a single night, but his hair turned white in the effort. The poem consists of two hundred and fifty columns of four words each. Mr. Giles gives the following, as a specimen of its style:—

> Like arrows years flow swiftly by;
> The sun shines brightly in the sky;
> The starry firmament goes round;
> The changing moon is constant found;
> The heat remains the fuel spent:
> Be then on time to come intent;
> A dignity of mien maintain,
> As if within some sacred fane,
> Adjust your dress with equal care
> For public or for private wear,
> For all men love to crack a joke
> At ignorant or vulgar folk.
> Four words, which give a sentence force,
> Are *really, so, indeed, of course.*

The Sacred Edict is often taken up next. The sixteen maxims which form the groundwork of this book were delivered in an edict by the Emperor Khang Hi in the latter part of his life. These maxims, each containing seven words, are often seen written on the walls of public offices. The son of Khang Hi, thinking to make their meaning more clear, wrote them out more verbosely, and later on a celebrated Salt Commissioner, Wang-yew-po, wrote a paraphrase of the whole book, simplifying the style. Thus amplified and simplified, they fill three hundred pages duodecimo. The following translation of the original maxims is by W. Milne :—

1st.

Pay just regard to filial and fraternal duties, in order to give due importance to the relations of life.

2nd.

Respect kindred, in order to display the excellence of harmony.

3rd.

Let concord abound among those who dwell in the same neighbourhood, in order to prevent litigation.

4th.

Give the chief place to husbandry and the culture of the mulberry-tree, in order to procure adequate supplies of food and raiment.

5th.

Hold economy in estimation, in order to prevent the lavish waste of money.

6th.

Magnify academical learning, in order to direct the scholar's progress.

7th.

Degrade strange religions, in order to exalt orthodox doctrines.

8th.

Explain the laws, in order to warn the ignorant and obstinate.

9th.

Illustrate the principles of a polite and yielding carriage, in order to improve manners.

10th.

Attend to the essential employments, in order to give unvarying determination to the will of the people.

11th.

Instruct the youth, in order to prevent them from doing evil.

12th.
Suppress all false accusing, in order to secure protection to the innocent.

13th.
Warn those who hide deserters, that they may not be involved in their downfall.

14th.
Complete the payment of the taxes, in order to prevent frequent urging.

15th.
Unite the tithings, in order to extirpate robbery and theft.

16th.
Settle animosities, that lives may be duly valued.

The student next takes up The Four Books, the standard text-books of all the schools, forming a complete curriculum for those who compete in the great examinations. These are—1st, *The Great Learning*, a treatise on government, written by an unknown author about five hundred years before Christ; 2nd, *The Doctrine of the Mean*, relating to motives in human conduct, and ascribed to the grandson of Confucius; 3rd, *The Discourses of Confucius*, containing almost all that is known of the life and teachings of the sage; 4th, *The Discourses of Mencius*, including his conversations with pupils and princes.

These books are all committed to memory, and their style is the criterion for all other writings. To use characters as they are used in these classics, is literary excellence. Many years are spent in acquiring this skill, and many men study till they are grey-headed without attaining it.

The oldest books are the semi-historic records which begin 2952 B.C. The Shu-king, or Book of History, relates to the reign of Yu, beginning 2357 B.C., and was

Language, Literature, and Folk-Lore.

compiled by Confucius in the sixth century B.C. from ancient historical documents then extant. It contains what is left of the early history of China, down to 720 B.C. Besides these histories, works are to be found in Chinese libraries upon every subject treated by authors in other lands. I find in a catalogue of books belonging to the Royal Asiatic Society the following works :—

Fifteen works on history, including one in 67 volumes, by the distinguished commentator Choo-fu-chu.
Lives of eminent men and celebrated females, in 120 volumes.
Biographical sketches of eminent females, in 8 volumes.
Eleven poetical works, consisting in all of 123 volumes.
A general outline of plants, in 43 volumes. This is considered the best pharmacopœia as well as the best botanical work in China.
Seven works on natural history, including an account of an island whose inhabitants are all women; of a country whose people have holes through the chest, permitting convenient transportation on a pole; of a region where headless human creatures have their eyes, noses, and mouths on the breast; and of flying swine and snakes with feet.
Twenty-eight works on Moral Philosophy.
Works on Metaphysics and Law. In the latter is a portion of the present legal code, giving this method of proving whether there be consanguinity between two men. Take a drop of blood from each, and drop these simultaneously on the surface of water in a cup; if the two drops mingle in sinking, then there is kinship between the two persons, but if they sink without mingling, or tend toward opposite sides of the cup, there is no blood-relationship between the parties.
Among works of fiction, one of the most popular is "The Dream of the Red Chamber," a novel in 20 volumes; and another is "Heaven's Rain and Flowers," in 30 volumes.
A hundred comedies of the Yuen dynasty, in 40 volumes, furnishes laughter for leisure hours.
The second emperor of the Ming dynasty appointed a commission of scholars to collect in one body all the classical, historical, philo-

sophical, and literary works hitherto published, embracing Astronomy, Geography, the Occult Sciences, Medicine, Buddhism, Tauism, and the arts. This work, executed by five chief and twenty sub-directors, with 2,169 subordinates, contained in all 22,877 books, beside the table of contents, which occupied 60 books more.

The Emperor Khang Hi, second of the present dynasty, who reigned sixty-one years, covering the end of the seventeenth and the beginning of the eighteenth centuries, caused to be published under his personal supervision the following compilations, known as the four great works of the present dynasty.

1st. A huge thesaurus of extracts, in 110 thick volumes.

2nd. An encyclopædia, in 450 books.

3rd. An enlarged and improved edition of a herbal in 100 books.

4th. A complete collection of the important philosophical writings of Chu Hi, in 66 books.

In addition to these, this Emperor designed and gave his name to the great modern lexicon of the Chinese language, which contains over 40,000 characters under separate entries, accompanied by citations from the works of authors of every age. Its compilation occupied thirty literary men five years.

Of the bulk of Chinese literature much has, during the present century, been translated into European tongues, opening to us a way of access to the thoughts of a vast people that have occupied a portion of the habitable earth longer than any other single portion has ever been occupied by one people. But no important addition to the sum of Western knowledge has been gained from this literature. For hundreds of years the Chinese have discovered nothing, invented nothing, improved nothing.

Books are so cheap as to be within reach of all. A copy of the trimetrical classic, with thirteen leaves, costs a halfpenny, and a volume of Confucius, with thirty-six leaves costs a penny. Sets of books in wooden covers, largely illustrated, and in the best style of the bookmaker's art, cost eight or twelve shillings. A book called

"Exhortations to Morality" is printed and gratuitously distributed as a Buddhistic work of merit. One of these, given to me by a native tract-distributor, has a preface which says that if this book be carried in a boat, the wind will be favourable and the waves will not be high; if kept on the person of a traveller, he will meet no robbers, and though he walk a thousand miles he will feel neither heat, cold, nor thirst; if laid up in a house, the demons will all withdraw from the dwelling; if read by a woman, she will bear five sons and two daughters; if read by a man, he will attain a literary degree; and all who ponder it carefully will have the length of his life doubled. After this series of falsehoods, the book proceeds to exhort its readers to practise truthfulness and other virtues.

The colloquial dialects are as unlike each other as are the various languages of Southern Europe. A company of seven men from Peking, Shanghai, Ningpo, Foochow Swatow, Canton, and Hakka highlands, would be unable to communicate with each other in oral speech. The Mandarin dialect is spoken in the northern and western provinces, by probably half the people of the empire, the Shanghai dialect by about thirty-four millions, and the Swatow dialect by perhaps six millions. Within the region over which a single dialect is used, there are such differences of pronunciation as to make the speech of one town unintelligible in another, and there is often great unlikeness in the vocabulary of two neighbouring villages. But with a single written and seven spoken languages one may communicate in China with a third of the population of the earth, while in order to reach the other two-thirds of the human family one must know 3,063 languages. The English language reaches less than a hundred millions of people, while the Mandarin dialect is used by perhaps two hundred millions.

One of the primary difficulties met by the learner of a Chinese dialect lies in the tones, which vary for the same syllable, giving the word diverse meanings according to the manner in which it is pronounced. There are four tones in the northern dialects and eight in the southern. At Swatow, *see*, evenly enunciated, means a corpse; *see* in a high key means a spoon; *see* with a falling slide means to die; *see* with a rising slide means to be; *see* with a questioning intonation means mankind; *see* in a low key means catsup; *see* abruptly spoken in a medium key means to flash; and *see* abruptly spoken in a high key means to consume. *Taw* is a knife, a cluster, a pocket, or the floor, according to the tone in which it is uttered. Of course misunderstandings must be frequent in a language in which *wa* in one key means a saddle, and in another key means a bowl; and where *tong* in a low tone means satin, and in a high tone means sugar; and where *too* with one inflection means a hoe, and with slightly different inflection means a hog.

Little accidents often arise from mispronunciation; such as happened at Swatow to a foreign housekeeper who sent her cook to buy tree strawberries, and was surprised to see him return bringing a sheep's tail; the difference between the names of the two articles being merely that between *ie bûe* and *ie bûe:* or such as happened in North China to a young missionary lady eager to be spiritually useful to the people, who began, after a few months' study of the language, to teach a class of boys in a Sunday School. She was telling the boys about King David, and referred to his having once slain a lion. She found that the boys were not impressed as she expected by this evidence of David's courage, and was a little surprised after the class was dismissed by overhearing one of the boys saying to another, "I do not see that David was so very brave in killing that creature; I myself have killed a great many of them." On careful reconsideration of what she had said she discovered that *shai* meant a lion but *shăi*, as she had said it, meant a louse.

Peculiar articulate sounds and singular idioms, add to the difficulty of acquiring the language; but as there is no conjugation of verbs nor declension of nouns to be mastered, it is, on the whole, with the helps that have been made for students, not more difficult to learn a Chinese dialect than to learn German or Spanish.

The masses of the people do not know how to read, but there exists among them an extensive folk-lore, which affects their character, conduct, customs, and thoughts. The wisdom acquired by experience is accumulated and communicated in proverbs, of which every man is as full as the servant of Don Quixote. Some of our own proverbs are repeated, such as "Misfortunes never come single;" "If the blind lead the blind, both fall into the ditch;" "Man proposes, Heaven disposes;" "Do as you would be done by;" "Practice makes perfect." Our saying, "Necessity is the mother of invention," is paralleled by their "Need breeds device;" our "Haste makes waste," by their "Urgent spinning makes bad yarn;" our "If you mount a horse, you must ride him," by their "He who bestrides a tiger finds it hard to dismount;" our "Pot calling the kettle black," by their "Tortoise laughing at the turtle for having no hair;" our "Looking for a needle in a hay-stack," by their "Dredging the sea for a pin;" our "Handsome is that handsome does," by their "Looks are born in the heart." They say, "Tinder should not be stored near a fire;" "A red-nosed man will be considered a drunkard whether he taste wine or not;" "Cutting off the nose does not remedy a bad odour;" "A sluice that does not perform its office is a cess-pool;" "When the mule is beaten, the horse is frightened also;" "It is hardly worth while playing the guitar to an ox;" "If you cannot have the dumpling, it is something to have the soup in which it was boiled;" "Sin is the root of sorrow;" "Right heart need not fear evil seeming." An improvident man is spoken of as one who waits till he is thirsty before digging a well; a prudent man as one who waits to see his guest before spreading his feast; an unreasoning man as one who cuts down a tree in order to catch the bird perched on its branch, or as one who breaks up his furniture in order to kill the rat concealed therein.

The public story-teller may be seen by the street-side or under an awning in an open area, narrating popular tales to a crowd of by-standers who throw into his tray a few *cash*, expressive of their pleasure in his recital. The Chinese have no firesides, but in the glimmer of the evening lamp, consisting usually of a saucer of peanut-oil with a bulrush pith in it as a wick, many stories not found in books are told to the delight of young and old.

CHAPTER XXXV.

THE SPHERE OF WOMEN'S WORK IN CHINA.

FEW Christians will dispute the need of male missionaries in China, but some do not see that a large number of female labourers is also required. While women here are far from possessing the freedom enjoyed by women in Christian lands, they are not life-long prisoners in zenanas as are the women of India. Taking into account the fact that a woman here incurs danger of extreme suffering if she confesses Christ without her husband's permission, while she is so supported by public opinion that she may safely oppose his wishes and follow all heathen practices if he be a Christian, it is remarkable that there are many female converts in missions where there are no ladies among the missionaries. Ten years ago nearly half of the two hundred native Church-members connected with this mission were women at country stations where no evangelistic work had been done by foreign ladies. The membership is now fourfold what it then was, and ladies have been largely engaged in special work among the native women; but the proportion of male and female members remains the same. In the English Presbyterian Mission here also, there were many female converts, even when there were no foreign ladies in the mission. It cannot therefore be said that missionaries of their own sex are absolutely necessary for making the gospel known to the women of China.

On the other hand, female labourers are almost as influential in adding men to the Church as they are in leading women to become Christians. The work of the Bible-women here has indirectly caused the turning of many men from idolatry. I have never had reason to doubt the willingness of Chinese men to receive instruction from a woman whom they believed to be a competent teacher, nor their docility under the guidance of a woman whom they respected. My conviction is, that the Chinaman's contempt for women is merely an incidental notion founded on his habitual experience of women's ignorance, and that he succumbs at once without regard to sex under the direction of one in whom he believes he has found wisdom. I do not doubt that there are in China many women who could successfully educate native preachers and superintend their work. We remember Mrs. Thomas, who has for many years directed the labours of fifty-two Karen preachers in the field where she was left alone at her husband's death; and Mrs. Ingalls, who has done both her husband's work and her own during twenty years of widowhood in Burmah. These instances show with what manful bravery and wisdom women may act when Providence gives them men's work to do. Providence may rightly set a woman in a position where human creatures would have no right to place her. Because remarkable tact and power are sometimes manifested by women under remarkable circumstances, it does not follow that the resulting success suggests a system which would be wise and safe for general adoption. The necessity for both male and female labourers in our missions arises out of just and

The Sphere of Women's Work in China. 205

common ideas of propriety and expediency, and not out of an impossibility that missionaries of either sex could do the work alone.

A mission would seem to be ideally complete when the number of workers of each sex was equal, and each worker was giving his strength to work among those of his own sex. God has so linked the fate of the two sexes, that the interests of the one can never be severed from those of the other. Whoever would elevate the one must provide for the advancement of the other also. Adam and Eve will always abide together, whether as inhabitants of Eden or as exiles outside. A worker for women will give large-hearted consideration to the true welfare of men; and a really successful helper of men will earnestly co-operate with those who work for women. God has made the well-being of each sex to depend largely on that of the other, and no one who ignores this truth in his plan of work will be a strong helper of human kind.

A true-hearted, right-minded, and capable woman can probably in any land render more real service to the needy of her own sex than can any man. In China this is more true than in some other countries, because of the distrust and scandal that at once arises among the heathen concerning any native woman who associates in any manner with men who are not her own kith and kin. Only those who know the grossness of the heathen mind, and the alacrity with which it jumps to evil conclusions, can understand how apt it is to traduce Christian women who depart from native customs, or how much the true interests of our work suffer if there be a lack of distinctness in the separation between its male and female departments.

As half the population of China is female; as this portion of the population is by far the more ignorant, oppressed, and sorrowful; as less than half the working force of missionaries are women; and as the ability of the native women and the customs of the country permit an extensive and effective employment of trained native female labourers, there seems to be reason why the lady missionaries in China should devote themselves exclusively to work among those of their own sex. This generation is passing away, and its opportunity to accept the gospel will soon be gone. The past and the future generations are in the hands of God, the present only is ours. If we see to it that the present generation is instructed in the way of the Lord, we may hope that the next will walk therein. Chinese mothers will influence the lives and characters of their children far more than any foreign missionary can. If we gain the wives and mothers of this generation we shall have almost secured the next.

As time goes on, the need of work done by women for women will be more and more felt in our missions; and as the number of lady missionaries increases, the question as to what is the exact relationship between their work and that of the male missionaries will become more pressing. The cause of woman's right has suffered greatly by having seldom had happy women as its advocates. A spirit of helpfulness ought to be the outcome of happiness. It is because my relationships in my work have been pleasant that I hope my experience may be of value to others. During the years that I have been training, using, and working with native female evangelists at Swatow, there has been no friction between my work and that of my associates, Dr. Ashmore and

The Sphere of Women's Work in China. 207

Mr. Partridge, who have been training, using, and working with native preachers in the same field, at the same country stations, and with similar methods and aims. Our work has been everywhere conterminous, but there has never been a question about boundaries. Our views coincided in the beginning in regard to the fundamental principles of missionary operations, and we agreed that the supervision of male helpers would remain with the male missionaries, and that the direction of female helpers would rest with me. I have very frequently needed the co-operation of the native preachers and the laymen of the Church in the carrying out of my plans for work among women; and on every such occasion the help asked for has been abundantly rendered under the advice of the missionary in charge of the work among men at that station. The hearty goodwill of the gentlemen in the mission toward the work attempted in behalf of the native women has diffused itself throughout the whole body of native Church members, and made that work possible and valuable.

There has sometimes been special work that could best be done by some special woman of the Church, and in all such cases the missionary has applied to me for the aid of my native female coadjutors. While we confer fully and freely with each other in regard to the interests of the work, the decision as to what shall be done in each separate case rests with the one who has charge of the department in which it lies, and that decision is accepted by the others as right and final. There is nothing more conducive to good fellowship and liberality than the certainty that one's rights will be scrupulously respected. So, while the pastoral care of the Churches as such devolves solely upon the ordained missionaries, the selection, education, employment, and superintendence of the female Church members in their work as evangelists, the supervision of female schools, and the care of native Christian and heathen women in general, is left unreservedly in the hands of the lady missionaries. Later comers of both sexes have cordially endorsed this plan of work; and we see no indication that it will not prove as good for the future, when there will be many missionaries, as it has in the past, when there were but few.

Every reason seems to be in favour of this division of labour and responsibility, while there are none that weigh against it in a well manned and well womaned mission. It not only accords with Chinese notions of propriety, which it is of no slight importance to have on our side, but also with enlightened Christian common sense and good taste.

www.ingramcontent.com/pod-product-compliance
Lightning Source LLC
Chambersburg PA
CBHW031815230426
43669CB00009B/1152